D0986925

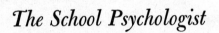

The School Psychologist

THE LIBRARY OF EDUCATION

A Project of The Center for Applied Research in Education, Inc.

G. R. Gottschalk, Director

Categories of Coverage

I	II	III
Curriculum and Teaching	Administration, Organization, and Finance	Psychology

IV	V	VI
History, Philosophy, and Social Foundations	Professional Skills	Educational Institutions

The School Psychologist

PAUL E. EISERER

Professor of Education
Teachers College, Columbia University

1963
The Center for Applied Research in Education, Inc.
Washington, D.C.

LIBRARY OF CONGRESS
CATALOG CARD NO.: 63-13292

PRINTED IN THE UNITED STATES OF AMERICA

Foreword

Some years ago, a practicing school psychologist said that he had worked for several years in a school system before he felt comfortable when teachers referred to him as the "school psychologist." Up to this point he had regarded himself as a psychologist working with school children. The broad conception of the potential contribution of the school psychologist which Professor Eiserer has projected in this monograph places the psychologist squarely within the school as a social institution, and gives an exciting picture of his involvement in its mission.

School psychology is an emerging profession. It is in fact so new that it has but a meager literature; psychology has not yet developed a model for its services to the schools, nor have teachers or school administrators come up with anything like a consensus with respect to the utilization of this new member of the team. Professor Eiserer has written with great clarity about these problems, and has set forth the many possible contributions which the psychologist can make to the improvement of educational services for all children. Without minimizing the assessment role in his work, the broad, creative aspects of the school psychologist's involvement in the processes of education are emphasized.

Professor Eiserer has written for the teacher and administrator, as well as for the school psychologist. Board of Education members too will find in this discussion the many ways in which the school psychologist can promote pupil growth and understanding. This is a timely monograph, devoted to an overview of an important profession.

MERRILL T. HOLLINSHEAD
Professor of Educational Psychology
New York University

Contents

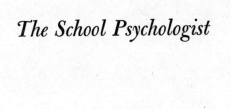

The School Psychologist

CHAPTER I

Emergence of School Psychology
as a Profession

When a teacher or administrator thinks about the school psychologist as a professional person, a number of questions may come to mind.

> What are his functions or roles?
> What kind of training does he have?
> Is he recognized as a qualified worker in schools through certification?
> How does his work relate to other specialists employed in the schools?
> How does he work with children, teachers, administrators, and parents?

Although the questions are reasonable, they cannot be answered with assurance. School psychology as a profession is so new and its representatives in different school systems often function so differently that the teacher or administrator may well wonder how this profession has come to be, and how it stands in relation to their own better established roles.

It is the aim of this book to deal with these questions and concerns of the educator and intelligent layman. In the course of this effort it should become clear that school psychology as a profession is newly born and is struggling with the problems of growing up. It has aspirations not yet fully realized, and some of these ideals are discussed in later chapters.

The answers to many of the questions stated above depend upon local circumstances. All of the roles for school psychologists described herein will not be found in every, if indeed in any, particular school system or community. This lack of uniformity is a fact of life for an emerging profession. Although the diversity of roles played by school psychologists today may appear confusing at times to the educator and layman, it is my view that this very diver-

sity offers opportunities for persons outside the profession to participate in the processes which will eventually lead to greater uniformity
in the conceptions, training, certification, and functions of school
psychology.

Until recently very little was known in a systematic way about
school psychology as a profession. To fill this void, a nationwide
conference was held in 1954 at the Hotel Thayer, West Point, New
York. The report of the conference proceedings was later published
and has popularly come to be known as the Thayer Report.[1] It is the
best single reference about the varied problems confronting a new
profession and provides information which serves as a basis for observing future developments.

Historical Antecedents

Educators have always been confronted with children of limited
mental ability and with children whose behavior presented difficulties which could not be handled in the regular classroom. Prior to
1900, problems of identification and placement for special instruction pointed to the need for special knowledge and techniques. It
was not surprising that the infant science of psychology was stimulated to meet these needs.

Studies of individual differences had already begun in Europe
under Galton, and child study had already become a field of systematic inquiry in the latter part of the nineteenth century. At the
turn of the century Binet was given the practical task of devising
intelligence tests for children. His success initiated one of the most
significant contributions of psychology to practical affairs: the development of tests to measure ability, aptitude, and achievement.
The testing movement has had far-reaching consequences on education in the United States. And school psychologists have been, and
remain, among the first to use such tests to deal with a wide variety
of educational problems.

In 1896 Witmer established the first psychological clinic which
focused on the learning problems of children. In 1899 the first public school department of child study was established in Chicago.

Another major historical influence was the emergence of the

---

[1] Norma E. Cutts, ed., *School Psychologists at Mid-Century* (Washington, D.C.:
American Psychological Association, Inc., 1955).

mental hygiene movement in 1908. From the start there was recognition of the significance of the childhood period in the development of behavior disorders. Community education programs over the years have stressed the importance of reaching children through the schools to identify and treat incipient disorders and—hopefully—to prevent them, if possible. The extraordinary development of child guidance clinics, which is still expanding, was a major result of this nationwide citizens' movement.

The influences which created the demand for psychological services in the schools were greatly intensified at the end of World War II. A new sense of urgency is found in the community (as well as in educational circles) that the quality of learning for all children and youth be improved wherever possible. The demand for special educational services for particular groups such as the retarded, the handicapped and disabled, the emotionally disturbed, and the gifted has been breathtaking. Trained personnel have frequently not been available to fulfill the aspirations of society and manpower shortage is at present a major problem in all the mental health professions. School psychology is no exception.

School psychologists apply the principles and techniques of psychological science to educational problems in a school setting. The particular knowledge available for application at any time depends upon the growth of the basic science. As psychology has grown during this century, it has become differentiated into a variety of applied professional disciplines, each of which draws upon substantive areas of knowledge in different ways to deal with the problems at hand. For example, knowledge about motivation and learning, individual differences, adjustment and behavior deviations, corrective and therapeutic procedures, behavior in groups, measurement and evaluation, and human growth and development represent areas of specialized knowledge within psychology. Applied psychologists, such as school, industrial, clinical, and social psychologists, draw upon these various specialized areas to fashion the particular principles and techniques appropriate to the tasks before them.

We can see, then, that two factors influence the principles and techniques to be used by any specialist: (1) the total knowledge available to him, and (2) the particular principles and techniques which are most relevant to his tasks. One would expect then that over a period of time, as knowledge expands—or at least changes, application will change. And this has been true in school psychology since 1900.

The other major historical forces shaping the roles of school psychology are, broadly conceived, the goals of the educational enterprise. As the focus of education has shifted from a set of limited purposes for a select group of students to a more comprehensive conception for the population as a whole, there have been corresponding changes in the problems faced by teachers and administrators. For example, provisions for individual differences and problems of motivation, learning, and adjustment have probably increased the range and complexity of the tasks faced by the schools. As a result, there has been a great increase in the demand for specialized services in the schools to assist teachers and administrators to realize more adequately the fundamental task set before them by society: to provide maximum opportunity for the greatest development of each and every pupil. Never has our society expected so much from the schools.

Certainly these two major influences have interacted upon one another. New knowledge about the range, variety, and patterns of human abilities and talents has influenced the formulation of educational philosophy and purpose even as it has provided some of the means by which such ends might be attained.

Here, however, in broad scope, it is emphasized that the roles of school psychology over the years have been shaped both by the advancement of psychology as science and profession and by the changing nature of educational philosophy and purpose.

Need and Availability of School Psychologists

Reliable estimates of the total number of psychologists employed in schools are not available. We do, however, have some idea of the growth of school psychology.

In 1948 the Division of School Psychologists of the American Psychological Association reported 88 members; by 1962 the number had increased to 820. Moreover, surveys have found that for every two school psychologists who were members of APA, there are three others who were not.[2] In 1958 the Department of Education in New Jersey reported that the number of psychologists with full-time employment had increased within the previous five years from 35 to 125.[3] New York State reported that 573 school psychologists were employed in that state in 1958.[4]

The apparently phenomenal increase in the number of school psychologists in so short a time is impressive, yet it can be deceptive. If we take the APA estimate seriously, we might assume that there are about 2000 school psychologists in the entire country. Assuming that the total school enrollment from kindergarten through high school was about 46 million in 1962, we would obtain a psychologist-to-pupil ratio of 1:23,000. Since the distribution of school psychologists over the pupil population is most certainly uneven, we may safely conclude that large numbers of pupils have no psychological services whatever available to them. In addition, few school systems which do have psychologists on their staffs would contend that a saturation point has been achieved in the use of services.

These data lead naturally to the question: What is the proper ratio of school psychologists to the pupil population? Since adequate service has not yet been defined and the nature of services has been expanding and varies widely, estimates are likely to be of limited use. However, they have varied from 1:1000 pupils to 1:3000. In the Thayer Report the latter figure was used in relation to a school population of approximately 45 million. On this basis there would be a demand for 15,000 school psychologists, an impossible requirement. Many examples come to mind where a school psychologist is serving on a full-time basis in a school with an enrollment of 500 pupils. No further figures are necessary to conclude that the supply falls far short of the demand.

Establishment of need for services is a complicated affair. The expansion of the demand in New Jersey came largely from state legislation requiring psychological evaluation to establish special classes for the mentally retarded. However, when school systems

2 Kenneth E. Clark, *America's Psychologists* (Washington, D.C.: American Psychological Association, Inc., 1957), p. 234.

3 New Jersey State Education Department, unpublished report (1958).

4 William A. Sivers, Jr. and Raymond Salman, *The School Psychologist in Action* (New York: The University of the State of New York, The State Education Department, 1961).

which had not had such services discovered that a competent psychologist's potential for service was not limited to such evaluations, they began to request additional and different types of assistance. Effective performance becomes the greatest impetus for expansion of services to other areas. No doubt this kind of event occurs frequently.

Training

A basic goal of the Thayer Conference was to assess the status and future needs for the training of school psychologists. Despite a growing need for psychologists in the schools, a deplorable lack of facilities for systematic training was noted. Most school psychologists were "self-educated" in the sense that they took work suggested by conscience or the specifications for certification required by a few states. The situation was one of laissez-faire, with only a few universities offering an explicitly defined training program. Although a number of universities have established training programs since 1955, reliable information about the extent of training facilities in the United States is not available.

A great deal of time and discussion at the Thayer Conference was devoted to the issue of levels of training. The problems involved, and the arguments pro and con, are given in this report. Consensus was achieved that school psychologists be trained and certified at two levels and general specifications for training at each level were recommended.

Although the aspirations of the conference and the general development of psychology in all fields make clear that the doctoral level of training will become the standard of the future, it is recognized that for quite awhile most school psychologists will continue to be trained at the one- or two-year graduate level. At the present time approximately 25 per cent of school psychologists hold the doctoral degree.

It is generally believed that level of training and the kinds of psychological service that can be offered are closely related. Until we have more definite studies of the relationship between kind and extent of training, and quality of performance, this general belief will be held and supported.

It is this writer's view that a single standard of training at the doctoral level is "the wave of the future" but not a realistic possibility in the next decade. The manpower situation in psychology suggests great competition for different areas of specialization within the field itself. A growing demand for services within the community and in the schools will operate to keep the predominant training level at about two years.

The question arises: What quality of professional performance is to be expected, given this reality? Developed competence, controlled by ethical considerations of responsible functioning within limits of training, assures that the schools will be reasonably served. Nevertheless, the schools will be better served when training and certification standards are upgraded.

Despite lack of systematic information about present-day programs for the preparation of the school psychologist, general comments about the nature of his training may be helpful. Most training programs recognize that the school psychologist must be trained in both psychology and education, with the greater emphasis on the theory and practice of psychology. The student usually acquires some knowledge of basic areas of psychology such as learning, human development, personality, measurement, and social behavior. He acquires theory and skills in the assessment and re-education of individuals and groups. An orientation in research helps him to interpret knowledge available to school personnel and alerts him to the necessity to evaluate his own procedures from time to time.

Since he works in an educational environment, he should be at home in educational philosophy, know the culture of the schools, have a working acquaintance with teaching methods and problems, and know how to work with other educational personnel to achieve the objectives of the school.

Although most of his training takes place in the classroom and clinic of the university, he may also serve an internship in schools, clinics, or hospitals.

The extent to which he acquires a depth and maturity in these areas of knowledge and skill will depend greatly upon the length of his training program. Although the student with two years of training may have achieved minimum competence in most of these areas, it is obvious that a psychologist with doctoral level training will have achieved higher levels of knowledge and skill.

Status of Certification Requirements

During the past two decades, several surveys of the certification standards and requirements for psychologists in the schools have been made, the latest by Hodges.[5] As of 1960, the situation is this: twenty-three states and the District of Columbia have some provision for certification; six more states, however, are in the process of establishing requirements. The trend is definitely toward an increase among the states and one may expect eventually that all states will certify psychological workers in the schools. Hodges reports that only four states specify the doctoral degree as desirable but these states also provide certification at lower levels. Six states require about two years of graduate study as the highest stage of certification. A majority of states specify the master's degree or equivalent as the acceptable level of training. And twenty-one states have neither specifications nor plans for the special certification of school psychologists!

A great diversity of conceptions governs the definition of certifiable training. In each state local influences apparently determine the specific areas and amount of training to be expected. Although there is evidence of some communality among the states which do have certification procedures in the important yet limited area of evaluation for special education, the great variety of patterns is not an encouraging feature. This view is predicated upon the premise widely accepted by psychologists that the psychologist should be firmly grounded in the essential theory and techniques of his science: "Psychologist first, school psychologist second."

There seems little doubt that specific certification standards have developed in response to specific pressures and views rather than out of the larger conceptions of psychology as a profession. This is not to say that existing standards have not been serviceable to schools or that they have been illegitimately evolved. These facts reflect some of the changes now going on within psychology and indicate how particular groups articulate their demands through governmental agencies. Also, the dynamic way in which the roles of school psychology are evolving suggest that a single standard of certification throughout the country is not an immediate possibility.

---

[5] W. L. Hodges, "State Certification of School Psychologists," *American Psychologist*, 15 (1960), 346–49.

It may be anticipated, however, that all persons with a stake in the matter—psychologists, educators, state agencies, and training centers—will continue to participate in the evolution of higher and probably increasingly uniform requirements.

Titles are interesting, beguiling, confusing. A study in 1950 indicated that psychologists in schools carried no less than thirty-eight job titles. This picture is changing, however, with a growing tendency (eighteen out of twenty-four states) to use the term *school psychologist* to designate the highest level of certification for psychologist in the schools.

The School Psychologist as a Member of the Educational Team

In all his activities, the school psychologist works cooperatively with other educational personnel. He rarely, if ever, functions alone. His essential task is to help the schools achieve their educational aims through application of psychological principles in particular situations. Such a function as the assessment of an individual child is possible only through cooperation with teachers, parents, and others. And effective remedial work is not possible without cooperative endeavor. In his consultative capacities the school psychologist often helps children indirectly by influencing the adults who work with them.

Frequently he also works together with other specialists in assisting teachers and administrators to fulfill their objectives. Reading and speech specialists, nurses, physicians, guidance counselors, social workers, and others participate with psychologists to constitute resources for special help when needed.

Thus skill for working in an interdisciplinary team are cardinal requirements for the school psychologist. The specific composition of the team is determined by the particular problems at hand. By the same token, the leadership role within a team at any time is best determined on the basis of function rather than status.

Although each member of the team, educator or specialist, has particular knowledge, insight, skills, and techniques based on his training and experience, there is also sufficient communality in background and purpose to make effective communication possible. To be sure, some jurisdictional disputes arise at times and questions of overlapping functions require clarification, but one must not lose sight of the unifying purpose achieved by the fact that each discipline draws upon the various sciences and arts to build particular professional competence. Thus, for example, all levy upon psychological science for knowledge and skill, but in different degrees, and all subscribe to a common educational purpose for the child, yet contribute in different ways to its accomplishment.

Looking Ahead

The chapters which follow will describe in nontechnical language the roles which school psychologists are playing or might play in the schools of today. No attempt is made to say what these roles should be and any effort to specify what roles *are* being fulfilled must be accompanied by an acute awareness of the rapid changes now occurring in the field. Few, if any, individual psychologists fully implement all of these roles. It is hoped, however, that an awareness of ideal possibilities will lead to an appreciation of the directions in which present conceptions are heading.

Although forces are at work which will result in greater uniformity of conception, training, certification, and function in the profession, it is hoped that teachers, administrators, and citizens generally will play a significant part in shaping the course of school psychology.

CHAPTER II

Factors Influencing and Limiting
the Roles of School Psychologists

Before discussing specific roles of school psychologists, it may be useful to consider some of the influences which define and delimit roles in particular situations. These roles are determined by a variety of factors which are continuously influencing one another.

The Community

It is axiomatic that the schools reflect the dominant values, aspirations, defects, and limitations of the community. It is also widely accepted that the schools should improve the welfare of individuals and the community. Both the conservative and the ameliorative aspirations of the school influence the ways in which psychologists are asked to contribute to educational goals. Communities with limited aims will use a narrower range of psychological services than those which set comprehensive goals for all children and are concerned with their intellectual, social, and emotional development.

Community characteristics associated with favorable psychologist-pupil ratios have not been studied in depth. But we may speculate about some of the factors that affect the quantity of psychological services and the ways in which the services are used.

School systems with higher expenditures per pupil are likely to employ more personnel services. The cost factor has also been shown to be positively correlated with defensible criteria of educational quality.

Other factors come to mind. Favorable attitudes toward the mental health professions, including psychology, and the use of mental health services for a wide spectrum of problems are associated with higher levels of educational attainment in the community. In all probability these various factors suggest that the socio-economic wellbeing of the community is a basic consideration in the demand for and use of psychological services both to improve educational quality and to meet mental health needs.

The importance of community mental health resources in assisting the school to achieve its mission will be considered later. Suffice it here to point out that the remedial potential of the schools will be affected by the community supply of assisting agencies.

The recent nationwide study, *Community Resources in Mental Health,* demonstrated considerable inequality in the distribution of such resources.[1] Although public resources tended to correct imbalances due to economic factors, the total supply and use were related to wealth factors. Some counties in this country have no resources whatsoever.

Other considerations, about which we have little reliable evidence, also influence the existence and use of school psychology. In the complex of suburban communities surrounding the inner city, one finds—side by side—a community with one psychologist for every 2000 pupils and another with none or one for 10–25,000 pupils. Penetrating field studies, yet to be made, might disclose why such differences occur. Available data suggest that the ratio of psychologists to pupils is less favorable in the very largest cities than in communities of middle size (25,000 or so).

The nature of the community will influence the kinds and variety of problems faced by the schools and consequently the ways in which psychologists will be asked to contribute to solutions. The relatively stable, homogeneous suburban community with intact family units finds more parents supporting and reinforcing the school's work than is the case in depressed, culturally deprived areas of the large city. There is great need for reliable epidemiological studies of behavior problems of school-age children and youth as related to a variety of community characteristics.

Specific cultural subgroups may present different traditions and attitudes toward psychological services in the schools. As school personnel relate to these groups or to persons within them, they must be alert to and respectful of the differences in receptivity and capacity to use services available to them.

---

[1] Reginald Robinson, David F. De Marche, and Mildred K. Wagle, *Community Resources in Mental Health* (New York: Basic Books, Inc., 1960).

It should be emphasized that extensive or intensive uses of services by a community does not suggest that it has more problems or more serious problems. It may reflect a community's awareness and desire to capitalize on the diversified resources of the science and profession of psychology to maximize potential educational development as well as to cope with problems of deviational behavior when such problems occur. It is a regrettable fact that many communities which appear to have great and urgent needs for services are unwilling or unable to obtain them.

In all communities which employ school psychologists it has been found that the demands for service exceed the supply. All current studies of manpower in the mental health professions strongly indicate that these shortages will continue for some time to come. As a result it may be expected that the better qualified persons will gravitate toward those communities which are able to support them well and provide the most professionally attractive work situation. Communities which offer wide scope for the deployment of trained ability will be favored.

The School

The school itself may be viewed as a social system with its own sets of expectancies, rewards, and punishments, and its own status levels for personnel. Subcultures for administrators, teachers (who may be clustered by grade levels or departments), special services personnel, and pupils are known to exist. The interactions among these groups, as well as among their members, constitute a complex of relationships within which roles of various personnel are defined. Communication networks—formal and informal—provide the matrix within which information and power are distributed.

Probably a sociological analysis would reveal interesting facts about the specific ways in which the above systems define the roles of the school psychologist. However, our interest here is in pointing to some of the ways that individuals influence whether and how psychological services are used.

Differences among the persons comprising school systems are tremendous with respect to attitudes toward psychology and psychologists, mental health and mental illness. Attitudes will range from very favorable to outright hostility or avoidance. The significance of individual attitudes lies ultimately in the fact that seeking or making use of services is a personal, voluntary decision.

If a principal has adverse attitudes toward psychology or toward a particular psychologist—for whatever reason—it is unlikely that such services will be widely or advantageously used in his school. A view based on unsatisfactory experience with an incompetent psychologist can be changed readily by working with a skilled one. However, views based on more irrational premises, such as uneasiness about clinical procedures or fear of disclosure when things go wrong in the school, are not so readily overcome. It is to be expected that the role of the psychologists will be restricted under these circumstances.

A principal who recognizes both the values and limitations of psychology and seeks to integrate them with total school resources for promoting educational development will soon generate a similarly open-minded, but critical, attitude within his faculty. This is one illustration of the power of an individual to exert pervasive influence on role functions within schools as presently organized.

As a more heterogeneous group, teachers vary more widely than administrators in attitudes toward psychological roles. More detailed examination of the dynamics of psychologist-teacher relationships will be made in subsequent chapters. Teachers are the chief consumers of service. They are the first to identify problems and are usually involved in their eventual solutions. Their attitudes and beliefs about the values of services determine whether or not they seek them and how they use them. Enormous variation is found among teachers in their readiness to seek help, in the kinds of problems for which help is sought, and in their capacity to make constructive use of assistance.

It may be stated that, in general, the climate for employment of school psychologists is most favorable at present. Administrators and teachers are increasingly desirous for the aid which psychology can give them in the discharge of educational tasks.

Often what is needed is competent demonstration of how psychology can be put to work in the service of schools. Not infrequently, a psychologist may be employed to perform a limited service—to evaluate children for special class placement, or to organize, administer, and supervise a group testing program. If the psychologist can do no more, his entire function may be defined within these limits. However, if he is more versatile, his colleagues will discover that he can helpfully do more. They may find themselves consulting him about behavior problems, learning difficulties, problems of group morale, and group problem-solving. Before long the demands on his services increase and his role expands.

The role of the psychologist will be affected by the functions of other special service personnel, such as guidance counselors, reading consultants, social workers, psychiatric consultants, and health specialists. Roles must be delineated, relationships worked out, and systems of communication established if effective team cooperation is to be expected. Since some of the training of these specialists has common elements, some roles may be interchangeable. Conflicts do arise but they can be resolved if the persons involved are inclined to work at them. Role assignment by functional competence within a flexible framework is a sound operational principle.

Training Programs

School psychologists are likely to practice what they have learned. If their training has been concentrated in clinical psychology with strong emphasis on diagnosis and psychotherapy, it may be expected that they will prefer such activities, that they will try to structure their school functions in those terms, and that they may conceptualize their roles as clinical psychologists working in the school. If their training has been limited to individual intelligence testing and psychometrics generally, they may seek to give substantial emphasis to these areas. Certainly there can be no objection to functions in either area for the schools have need of both. However, our thesis here is that most schools will be better served when psychologists are qualified to perform a diversity of roles.

Since organized training programs are in early stages of development, universities have not exercised a systematic influence in role definitions of school psychologists. Rather, they have been reacting to outside forces which asked for certain functions to be performed. Individuals have then sought to acquire the competence to perform these functions. In this sense the schools have led the way in expanding a concept of the potential role of psychology in education. Both the universities and the schools have a strategic role to play in fashioning the emerging profession of school psychology. It is very encouraging to note increasing recognition of the need for co-operative relationships between them. For example, selected school systems are already providing internships for students—in-service training which includes supervision and remuneration in coopera-tion with training centers. Such arrangements are proving to be mutually rewarding.

It was pointed out (see Chapter I) that the trend is toward train-ing school psychologists in two- or four-year programs, the latter leading to the doctorate. Probably more students are being trained today in one- or two-year programs than in four-year programs. In the shorter program, less attention can be given to theory and research. Training is geared toward preparing the student to per-form the more urgent functions required by the schools: the study of individual pupil problems and the classification of pupils in special education. This fact will certainly limit the role possibilities of the psychologist.

The psychologist can hardly be expected to essay roles for which he has little or no training—as in research and in consultant capaci-ties, for instance. For the present, at least, we have the paradox of the expansion of role expectations in the schools and the entrance of many persons in the field who cannot fulfill them.

Limitations on preservice training point to the urgency of con-tinuing professional education on the job. Realization of this need has been a potential factor in the development of professional as-sociations of school psychologists on local and state levels. A recent survey among such associations in New York, New Jersey, and Connecticut disclosed a surprising amount of such activity, initiated and executed by the associations. The survey also revealed that psychologists are responding to the challenges presented to them by the schools. It may be anticipated that this type of professional pro-gramming will increase with greater involvement of training centers and state departments of education.

Certification Requirements

It is difficult to assess with confidence the impact of certification requirements on role functions. Since one cannot readily infer from stated requirements the influences which determined them, specula-tions about intent will vary widely. If requirements exist, however, all school psychologists may be expected to meet them, thus giving recognition to a concept of some minimum qualifications. Unfortunately, minimum expectations are viewed as maximum by many persons.

In all states having requirements, certification for subdoctoral training is possible and is held by the great majority of psychologists. Although standards are being raised, the process is very slow and—in light of our high expectations—the situation might be viewed as most discouraging. Much time and considerable effort will be required before school psychology as a whole achieves the high level of professional competence represented by the doctoral degree.

Although certification requirements are viewed as one means by which a profession achieves maturity and provides some assurance of competence to the public, they also have a negative side. Codified requirements are often exceedingly difficult to change. The view taken here is that they are necessary and desirable and that the means for keeping them responsive to change must be contrived.

It is well-nigh impossible to know the state of affairs in states which have no certification requirements. Studies are greatly needed to determine the conditions which govern entry into the profession and the kinds and quality of roles performed. Where no state standards exist it may be surmised that, in effect, employing school systems serve as certifying agencies. The diversity of standards must surely be greater than those existing in the other states.

As we look ahead we may expect most states to adopt certification requirements and, in accordance with our traditions of states' rights, the level of training expected will be determined by what local conditions will support. National organizations of school psychologists, such as Division 16 of the American Psychological Association, will continue to perform an educational and advisory function.

There is also slowly emerging a closer cooperation between state departments of education and training universities. One desirable pattern is for state accreditation of training programs in which the graduate is certified upon completion of the training program. One criticism of certification requirements has been that they do not embody a clear and integrated concept of training, but represent an accretion of required courses emerging from fragmentary pressures over a period of time. In addition, without organized training programs which embody a training concept, most certification could be described as "self-certification." Thus the person seeking acceptance merely accumulates courses, often from diverse sources, as a way of meeting requirements.

Program certification holds the further promise that experimentation with methods of training may be possible—an obvious necessity in a new field if we are not to freeze training procedures prematurely. Perhaps it should be added that no arrangements or structures of relationships will guarantee imagination and constructive use of freedom.

Professional Self-Image

In considering the impact of institutional forces represented in the community, school, university, and state, we should not lose sight of the potentially significant part which the individual psychologist may exercise in defining his roles in the school. In some situations the psychologist merely reacts to what is expected of him, doing his best to fulfill the expectations of others. He takes the views of others as valid for him, or, if he recognizes them as valid and cannot meet expectations, responds with avoidance and inevitable professional frustration.

Another psychologist discerns areas for choice and decision within the context of his work. When more is expected than he can deliver, he seeks to determine priorities among functions. He actively participates with other school personnel in evaluating the ways in which he, with his particular competence, can best contribute to the educational effort. He does not hesitate to make his views known and is willing to risk his ideas in the arenas of decision-making. He not only responds to but accepts the challenge of leadership.

One psychologist may feel victimized by circumstances beyond his control; another may seek professional and self-fulfillment through partnership with others. The differences lie partly in the objective circumstances but perhaps more in the attitudes which he holds toward himself and his profession.

If a psychologist perceives his professional role as a limited one, he will seek to limit his actions accordingly. He may correctly perceive that roles are expected which are outside the boundaries of his competence and he is ethically required to limit his activity to areas of competence. If he has limited skills in research or therapy, he can defend his noninvolvement in them without seeking further training.

If a psychologist has more broadly trained capacities, but expectations of him are more limited, he has two choices. He may align his performance with expectations or he may work toward a role definition more congruent with what he can do.

Differences among psychologists faced with ostensibly comparable external circumstances cannot be understood except in personal terms. Yet psychologists, not unlike other persons, often seek the answers to their dilemmas in outer conditions. One of the important values in continuous involvement in programs of professional development is the ongoing scrutiny of all possible sources for growth. Continuing evaluation by the psychologist of his own professional image may be his greatest impetus for growth.

CHAPTER III

Assessment Roles

Surveys have repeatedly shown that the most frequently occurring activity of the school psychologist is the assessment of the abilities, aptitudes, interests, achievements, personality, and adjustment of individual pupils. Since he is probably the person on the school staff best trained in the theory and techniques of measurements of all kinds, he is called upon to provide leadership, guidance, and technical competence in situations where measurement contributes to educational objectives.

Principles and Concepts

Assessment depends upon some underlying theory of growth and development. The questions asked, the data collected and its evaluation, the remedial program—all acquire meaning in relation to some view of how persons develop in relation to their environment.

Our view here is that behavior is a complex function of the interaction of internal and external forces. The characteristics of the child—intellectual, emotional, physical, and social—help define an internal dimension which influences and is influenced by environmental forces. It is what we mean broadly by the term *personality* or *personal identity*.

The other dimension, the external, comprises the influences of people and culture upon the person. The individual's environment depends upon his perception of it as well as upon its own nature. The environment includes interpersonal relations—the significant persons in the home, the school, and the community who have some impact on the individual. It also includes the particular subculture in which he lives. Norms of behavior, roles, expectations, and systems of reward and punishment are set before the person, more or less clearly, by the subcultures to which he and his family belong. The individual can best be understood in terms of his personal

20

identity and in relation to the sociocultural milieu of which he is a part.

This view constitutes the background against which assessment acquires meaning. Any behavior or misbehavior is perceived as a function of a complex interplay of forces. A study of a child outside his milieu has severe limitations. Both personality and culture must be examined to obtain an adequate picture of the meaning of behavior.

The psychologist generally makes other assumptions in his assessment endeavors. He regards behavior as multicaused in most instances. Rarely does he expect to find a single cause for a behavioral event, whether it be an attitude, a value, a thought, or an overt action. One might say that he looks for the more probable causes of a particular event. He cannot with certainty say that A caused B. We may yearn for certainty but our ignorance will not allow it!

Behavior is also viewed as having current and historical dimensions. One's responses to present situations are always to some degree determined by a history of responding to similar (actual or perceived) situations in the past. The shaping influences of the past are the target of investigation in every case history.

These considerations are widely shared by psychologists. Furthermore, any individual psychologist operates within a particular theory of human growth and development. He may subscribe to psychoanalytic, behavioristic, self-, or biosocial theory as a framework for understanding children. It is not our purpose here to elucidate the characteristics of different theories, for discussions are readily available in the professional literature. Suffice it to remind ourselves that some theory is necessary and is more or less explicit to all of our efforts to understand and modify behavior.

For example, we commonly hear that a child behaves a certain way in class in order to attract attention. We may "explain" the behavior as a child's way of satisfying a "need for recognition." The concept of a "need for recognition" is part of a particular theoretical way of viewing behavior.

Sometimes difficulties in communication arise between psychologists and teachers, or among psychologists themselves, because they view behavior through different theoretical spectacles. Fortunately there is enough communality among theories to permit communication to occur at reasonable levels if the persons concerned work at it. Perhaps the most useful way to enhance communication is to focus, not on theories, but on the specific behavior of children to be comprehended. By maintaining our focus on the data, a surprising amount of common agreement can be reached about the "how" and "what" of behavior and the procedures bringing about change.

Let us then look at some of the practical concerns that are pertinent to any assessment approach. All such approaches begin with questions, for an explicit question is the starting point of inquiry. This does not mean that a formulated question is rigidly framed and unchangeable. But the psychologist should no more aimlessly assemble information about pupils or groups or situations than a geologist would gather pebbles on the beach without some guiding purpose. It is so easy and tempting to collect information as an end in itself that there is probably excessive data-gathering by many without a clear conception of the purpose for so doing. Time and thought given to the delineation of the purpose, problem, or question to be answered is the hallmark of expertise in this phase of the psychologist's work. He continuously asks himself: "What do I wish to know, and why?" Finding out everything that it is possible to discover about a person is a sign of the novice. Compilation of all kinds of data without informed purpose is wasteful of time and energy.

Thus the psychologist first addresses himself to the question. Often he works with a teacher, for example, to clarify the concerns she may have about a child's behavior. If a teacher observes, "There's something peculiar about Johnny's behavior," the psychologist discusses the peculiarities with her until the difficulty can be more clearly differentiated.

It is important to recognize that productive question formulation is a process, occurring over time until both persons are satisfied that a meaningful question has evolved. Only then can it be decided whether more data is required for successful resolution than is now at hand. Every psychologist has had the experience of starting with a teacher's vague formulation of concern about a student and as a result of mutual exchange of information has discovered there really was no need for additional data.

For example, a teacher may observe, "Johnny is performing poorly," and wonder why. Upon joint study of data available on

Johnny's performance in relation to his ability, it may be discovered that he is functioning adequately for himself but not as well as others of greater ability. The teacher may have forgotten, not had available, or misinterpreted existing data. The psychologist may help her remember, make data available, or reinterpret data in such a way that the initial question is answered.

On the other hand, the observation that Johnny is performing poorly may be based on existing information and the discussion may then lead to the preliminary formulation of some reasons why this may be so. The point is that the first step is to arrive at a clear formulation of questions before additional observations are made.

Diagnosis, then, is a process, not a single event. Question formulation includes the use of all existing data (records, teacher's observations) to determine what additional data, if any, are needed to resolve the problem. Psychologists sometimes rush prematurely into giving batteries of tests or interviewing others when such procedures are unnecessary or inappropriate, with the subsequent discovery that it is not the amount of information that is important but the quality and relevance of the data to clearly formulated questions.

Experience in diagnosis also reveals that it may be a progressive process. The answer to one question may lead to another question. For example, after it is ascertained that Mary is behaving outside the bounds of normal expectation, the next question may be "Why?" Because of the complexity of behavior and the great variety of theories extant, an almost unlimited number of questions *might* be formulated to guide the next steps in the inquiry. But, on the basis of all known data, *likely* questions (hypotheses) may be formulated. In a sense, then, the process continues to a point of mutual satisfaction to teacher and psychologist, to a point where action of some kind can be taken in relation to Mary.

Diagnosis is always action-oriented, another way of saying that it is purposeful activity. Data are not collected for their own sake, or merely for problematic future use. They are collected in the anticipation that some new action or attitude will ensue. Whether this process is called assessment, appraisal, diagnosis, or evaluation, its importance is apparent and is at the heart of much of the work of the psychologist.

Methods, Procedures, Techniques

Referral. Questions usually are brought to the attention of the psychologist through a process of referral. The referring person may be an administrator, a teacher, a guidance counsellor, or other personnel. The particular channels of referral are best worked out by the personnel in any given situation. The important point is that the procedure makes it possible for the teacher to receive help at the earliest possible moment. In discussing the more formal aspects of referral, it should not be concluded that informal consultations with teachers about pupils are unimportant.

The more formal procedures are usually initiated through use of a referral form. There is no "ideal" form. Basically, it is a way of initiating communication between the teacher and psychologist about a child. The form should be cooperatively evolved to serve the purposes of a particular situation.

The form should help the teacher formulate her ideas about the issues on which she would like assistance. It should encourage her to select and report descriptively the observations which underlie her concern. She may also make an initial formulation of the questions arising from these observations. *The form should be simple and short.* It should not require her to do clerical work in assembling data from school records. Such procedures discourage the use of psychological services.

The form should provide the psychologist identifying information about the child but, chiefly, inform him about the teacher's concern and the basis for it. Hopefully, it will suggest possible next steps for him. At the least it provides a common basis for a conference with the teacher, if such a conference is indicated. It might also suggest the need for additional observations prior to such a conference. He may wish to examine the school records, or his own files, before deciding upon his next steps.

It is important to recognize that if he is to function in a professional manner, his procedures must be flexible. His procedure may vary from case to case, or from teacher to teacher. A psychologist may proceed differently with a teacher with whom he has previously worked.

It cannot be overemphasized that the psychologist works in partnership with teachers and that the collaboration may take different forms with different teachers. Past experiences, present relationships, and different temperaments, backgrounds, and skills—all affect the form which the collaboration will take. Teachers have to learn how a particular psychologist may help them, just as the psychologist has to learn how to help particular teachers. To each his own! Working partnerships cannot be prefabricated.

Dynamics of referral. Many factors contribute to the teacher's readiness to use the services of the school psychologist. Among them are the teacher's objectives and aspirations in teaching, her knowledge of the growth and development of students, her sensitivity to behavioral variations and their significance, and her willingness to ask for assistance when things go wrong.

If a teacher sets as her main goal the training of the mind, she may not be alert to problems of emotional and social significance or may believe them to be irrelevant. Her knowledge of normative growth patterns will influence her judgment. Her own adjustment and feelings of security will aid or inhibit her in recognizing problems in others. She may be able to acknowledge problems of acting out aggression, or of flaunting authority or of behaving aggressively in verbal or physical assaults on others, while she views the more withdrawn pupil more as a source of satisfaction than a source of concern. Awareness of her own problems, too, may allow her to recognize the problems of others.

A teacher is more likely to refer problems if she recognizes her own limitations and does not view children's problems as necessarily a reflection upon her own competence. If she believes she is expected to deal successfully with all children's problems she will be reluctant to seek help. Also, if she feels on the basis of past experience that psychologists are not likely to be helpful she will keep her own counsel.

Every teacher must learn which problems she can successfully cope with herself and for which she requires outside help. There is no magic formula. One of the values of psychological services which are provided *through* rather than *for* teachers is the strengthening of the capacity of a teacher to deal with problems by herself. On the other hand, a teacher cannot test the limits of her own capacities if she does not do all that she can before seeking assistance. There is no easy way. Every teacher must strike a balance between asking for help with everything, thus inhibiting her own capacity for growth and developing a sense of inadequacy, and never referring problems because of a false sense of pride or omnipotence.

A moment's reflection about the enormity of the task confronting the teacher in today's schools and the complexity of human motivation and behavior should convince both teacher and psychologist that no one person is wise or omniscient enough to deal effectively with all problems. Each person has limitations as well as potential contributions to make. One of the irrational compulsions in modern education is that we ought to do a highly effective job with everyone. This is sheer nonsense when we recognize our collective ignorance or impotence in some situations. Yet we often fret about failures that are not the result of negligence but of lack of knowledge, skill, and everyday human frailty.

Referrals will also reflect the particular interests, competences, and skills of the psychologist. He cannot help where he lacks knowledge or diagnostic skill, or if he has limitations in human relationships. Some psychologists are abler, more sensitive, more skillful, more dedicated than others. This is, of course, true of any professional group.

Types of referrals. Experience has shown that many kinds of problems are referred to school psychologists for assistance. Difficulties in learning, behavior disturbances in the classroom, social deviations, and personality disorders represent commonly used classifications of problems. Teachers, of course, vary in skill in detecting difficulties in pupils and also in attitudes toward seeking assistance.

No simple formulae can be given to assist teachers in early identification of pupil difficulties. Because of her special competence in pupil learning, a teacher is most likely to detect problems in this area. Deficiencies in skills such as reading and arithmetic, or a mediocre academic performance or steady or sudden deterioration in performance by a pupil known to be capable of superior work may be readily noticeable to the teacher in the course of his daily work.

A highly recommended procedure is for the teacher or teachers to meet with the psychologist over a period of time for frank discussion about the kinds of problems which the teacher faces in her work. Within this framework each may learn about the interests and skills of the other and together they can formulate some working ideas concerning the kinds of problems which the teacher can competently handle by herself, those for which brief consultation may be appropriate, and those which may require more intensive individual study by the psychologist. Most teachers respond favorably to this cooperative approach, for within this mutual helping process misunderstandings may be minimized and professional growth for all concerned is a real possibility. Whether this kind of procedure occurs between two professional persons or in a group depends entirely upon the particular situation.

Much has been written about the difficulties or failures of teachers to identify the pupil problems which are not overtly expressed as learning deficiencies or behavior disturbances. The passive, shy, or withdrawn child may not be recognized as having problems of an emotional nature. However, mental health education in the community and in teacher training has improved the situation considerably. Moreover, if the kind of cooperative activity recommended here is carried on, the teacher will grow in her ability to identify a wider range of problems and to discriminate more sharply the kinds of assistance needed to cope with them.

In larger school systems where the psychologist-teacher ratio is unfavorable, other schemes have been devised. One such approach might be called "group screening." At a time when the teacher is reviewing the progress of each child for the report card, she might be asked to identify pupils who seem to be having particular difficulties—academic, emotional, social, or whatever. The list is then given to the psychologist for further study. There is no implication at this point that the difficulties are serious, but such a review assures that every child is given consideration. Minor difficulties, which could become major ones if not recognized, are often reviewed and discussed.

If this procedure were followed, there would be fewer instances in which a serious problem is identified, only to discover from pupil records that warning signals had been given over several years but had been ignored or considered too petty for serious attention.

If the procedure be considered too time-consuming, it should be pointed out that the investigation and remedial procedures required by serious difficulties may later take a tremendous amount of time. Lesser problems take less assessment and remedial time and prevent the development of a number of serious problems. And more pupils are served with the usually limited professional resources.

Criteria for teachers. Except that it is sometimes forgotten, it hardly seems necessary to remind ourselves of the enormously wide range of individual differences among teachers with respect to sensitivity, interest, knowledge, and skill in promoting the educational development of pupils. Nevertheless, every teacher is on the front line of defense when things go wrong in pupil growth.

Some teachers require help for problems which other teachers can handle by themselves. If a teacher considers her present competence from an historical viewpoint, she is likely to discover that she now successfully handles problems which at an earlier point in her experience required assistance or were not handled at all. While experience in problem-solving does not automatically make us wise and self-sufficient, it may certainly help.

What criteria may a teacher apply to help her make a decision to seek assistance? Some of the following suggestions may prove useful. Usually a teacher faces two dilemmas. First, is there a problem which requires more than the usual attention? Second, if a problem does exist, can she take care of it by herself or does she need assistance?

How may a teacher decide that a problem exists? Obviously, the teacher's knowledge of developmental norms at a given age, her personal sensitivity, her awareness of reasonable performance expectations for a given child, and other factors, influence her perception of pupil problems. The more she knows about the individual pupil and about her class group as a whole, the more discerning she will be. Generally speaking, she is alert to deficiencies in behavior whether they be in academic learning, social adaptation, physical vigor, or emotional maturity.

A deficiency obviously implies failure to achieve some standard or expectation, whether the norm be for the group or for the individual pupil. While it is true that no one functions at maximum efficiency all the time, and that variations in performance are to be expected, the teacher may well be concerned when deficiencies persist over a period of time.

A sudden or dramatic change in behavior may at times be indicative of trouble even if it is of short duration. Conclusions are not to be drawn at this point, but the teacher may become more vigilant to developments which may call for action.

It is not the objective here to describe the endless varieties of pupil behavior, but merely to suggest in general terms considerations which may assist the teacher from some normative viewpoint to recognize problem behavior in pupils.

In the normal course of teaching, problems are encountered and resolved. When a difficulty is identified, procedures to resolve it are initiated by the teacher. In a sense, it may be said that teachers spend a rather sizeable amount of time in such problem-solving activity. It is only when her own usual and best efforts are of no avail that the teacher considers asking for assistance from the psychologist.

This does not mean, as some people fear, that the teacher recognizing an obviously emotionally disturbed child in class should institute therapy in the classroom. She may recognize problems which immediately suggest to her that she has neither time nor skill to cope with them, and that require prompt assistance.

On the other hand, if teachers are not encouraged to help pupils solve problems, they will not develop their own capacity for better teaching. The problem of when to ask for help cannot be resolved by general formulae but only on an individual basis with due regard for the complex factors involved.

Classroom observation. One of the most fruitful ways for teachers to understand how psychologists work is to become acquainted with the techniques and procedures which they employ. In this connection it is important to realize that the psychologist selects from his repertoire of knowledge, skills, and techniques those which promise to be most helpful. He does not do the same thing in every situation.

Psychologists frequently make classroom observations, but for reasons that will differ from case to case. By visiting a classroom a psychologist can observe the larger context within which a child behaves. He gets some notion of the makeup of the class, of how the prospective client behaves in a group situation. This is helpful not only in providing desirable data about a child, but enables the psychologist to see the total situation within which constructive suggestions may be made after the study is completed. He may observe aspects of the child's behavior that have escaped the teacher's attention. Such observations may provide useful points for later discussion.

He may get some idea of the classroom climate in which the child is functioning, some idea about how other children react to the child, something about the relationship of the teacher to the child and to other children. He may not make a systematic analysis of the social structure of the class, as through sociometric devices, but he can acquire a general picture of the situation. If a psychologist has developed familiarity with a particular classroom and teacher over time, he may not make such observations in a particular case. That is why flexibility is essential in his procedures.

Interviews. Perhaps the most commonly used assessment procedure of the school psychologist is the interview. As a tool for collecting data it is employed with the pupil, principal, teacher, parent, and whoever may have information of potential use in assessment. Since numerous excellent descriptions of the aims and processes of interviewing are available to the interested reader, no attempt will be made here to discuss them in detail. However, some aspects of special pertinence to interviewing pupils, teachers, and parents will be considered.

Although there are exceptions, the psychologist is likely to talk privately with the pupil after a referral has been made. Such an action should be a sign to the pupil that he has a significant part to play in the process getting under way. His perceptions of the problem situation will be given serious attention; he has information to offer which will help provide as comprehensive an understanding as possible; his cooperation is needed in any effort to modify a situation. He is not an object to be studied, analyzed and reformed. He is a person with difficulties who is invited to be an active participant in a helping process.

Not all pupils will perceive a referral to the psychologist in this happy light. The unwilling, resistant, uncommunicative pupil offers a challenge to the psychologist's skill. The resistance must be overcome, for the interview will not be very productive until some kind of cooperative relationship is established. Because the interview occurs in a school situation, the pupil may be apprehensive about the psychologist's intentions and uncertain as to whether information given will be held in confidence. Assurance of the confidential nature of the communication is essential to effective work, whether it be with pupil, teacher, or parent. When there are exceptions, the pupil should be told at the outset why the psychologist must be given freedom of judgment and action.

Occasions arise when the psychologist must state the nature of his function in the school. Uncertainty may exist in the eyes of pupils with respect to the authority of the psychologist to modify rules, change schedules, or intervene in administrative decisions. He has the obligation in such situations to state clearly the nature of his role and the limits of his authority and action.

With younger children a modified play-interview may be more appropriate for assessment purposes. A corner of the office may be equipped with materials for use by the child in expressing problems which he is unable or unwilling to express in words. Play activity with or without talk, finger painting, or drawing may provide data for understanding the problem. It is important here, as in all interviews, that an atmosphere be created in which the pupil can feel free and safe to reveal feelings, thoughts, fantasies, and ideas without fear of condemnation, judgment, or punishment. Limits are imposed only on action and overt behavior as the realities of the situation require.

Teachers. After a preliminary review of the referral request, and the acquisition of supplementary data if needed, the psychologist usually confers with the referring teacher.

How the interview is perceived makes a difference. If the situation is so perceived and structured that the psychologist is the expert interviewing or interrogating the teacher to obtain data about the child, each will have a certain attitude which will affect what data are selected and what will be done thereafter.

If the teacher and psychologist both view the conference as one in which they are joining efforts to accomplish a common task— that of helping a particular pupil—different consequences will ensue. The involvement and participation will have a different quality. Constructive collaboration is possible only through mutual respect. The teacher and the psychologist are experts in different areas. Each has something different to contribute and each has to learn what that contribution can be.

In the first situation the teacher sees herself as providing information for another's use. She may readily assume a dependent role, with minimum involvement: "Let the expert do it!" She may withhold data that she thinks will be damaging to herself, or that will make her behavior appear in an unfavorable light. Also, she may find herself making a minimal commitment toward a resolution of the difficulty. The inequality in the expert-dependent roles may well sabotage the effort or at best make it less effective than it could be.

When two persons, expert in different but equally essential areas, combine their skills in a context of mutual respect, a rather different quality of relationship follows. Defensiveness is reduced when neither has to prove himself. Expertness on each part is assumed and respected. The persons involved can get to the business of *sharing* information, doubts, queries, interpretations, puzzlements. The focus is on helping the child, not proving oneself. One doesn't worry about how good a teacher one is, or how good a psychologist. One simply does one's best to get the job done.

As the psychologist and teacher share their perceptions, identify areas of agreement, and review points of difference, an enlarged picture of the child often results. Each observer perceives the situation from a different background, attends to events that seem especially significant in the light of his own concern for the child. Thus each calls to the other's attention new data for the consideration of new hypotheses to understand the child's behavior. Frequently, the hypothesis which evolves is more comprehensive, as it encompasses more data, and leads to further fruitful exploration. This process is reciprocally satisfying and the resulting teamwork augurs well for the effective carrying out of any remedial procedures that may eventually be formulated.

A word is in order about the different orientations that the clinician and teacher frequently bring to the study of a child. If not properly understood, these differences may create difficulties in communication, or irritation and impatience. Under optimum circumstances, these differences can lead to a more comprehensive evaluation of the child than is possible for either one alone.

The clinician often seeks to understand the child's complete functioning, including antecedent events and influences; he is concerned with the symptomatic nature of surface behavior and with its underlying dynamics. He may focus on the aberrations rather than the more normal aspects of development. He wonders where the child will be heading if present behaviors go unmodified.

On the other hand, the teacher has a different aim: to educate the child and to do it in the context of a group situation. She is more concerned about helping him learn appropriate intellectual and social tasks, about his effective participation in the group. She may be concerned with pathology as it may interfere with more normal pursuits.

Although their orientations do indeed overlap, the psychologist and teacher will work better at their common task—the promotion of the educational fulfillment of the child—if they are sensitive to their differences and take them into account.

Parents. Not all problems referred to the psychologist require involvement of the child's parents. In most cases in which an intensive study of the child is indicated, however, the parent will be involved—and with good reason. Much data for understanding the child will just not be available from school records. A dynamic view of the developmental history, and the current situation in the family are not likely to be available. The only procedure available for obtaining such information is the parent interview.

One may safely assume that parents will approach such an interview with some apprehension. A stereotyped view of the school's interest in them as instigated because of "trouble" with the child will put them on guard. The telephone call may be a sign of their failure as parents. The reactions to these fears or fantasies will vary. One parent will respond with deference and helplessness. Another will become aggressive and defiant; typically the situation is emotionally charged for the parent, and the psychologist ignores this at his peril.

As with the teacher, the psychologist will progress best with the parents when he sees the exchange of views as one of genuine collaboration on behalf of the child. The child is the occasion for their coming together and if the focus is kept there a fruitful interview will result.

The parent, disturbed or not, has much to reveal which will enrich awareness of the child's behavior in school. All data offer illumination. A parent may be especially apprehensive during the psychologist's interrogation, fearful of having to disclose too much about family affairs. If the conversation can be structured around understanding and helping the child, the interview will be the more successful. Parents are bound to reveal more than they intend to and a sensitive interviewer will learn much about aspects of the home environment which are not directly discussed.

Another fundamental reason for establishing a mutually cooperative and respectful relationship with parents is that in most instances the parent will have a part in carrying out the remedial program that is finally developed. Not only is the psychologist interested in obtaining information that will help him to understand the child, but he is also seeking to gain an appreciation of the parents' willingness and capacity to contribute to the remedial program.

Tests.   Frequently the psychologist will administer standardized tests. The test or battery of tests given depends upon the purpose at hand. A battery of tests is no substitute for clear thinking about the kinds of questions to which these tests may provide relevant data. There may be some truth to the frequently stated suspicion that too many tests are given in school these days. Tests are tools to be used after it has been determined that they may provide pertinent information about some specified issue.

Selected tests may also be used for an exploratory purpose, when the psychologist is looking for leads to an understanding of a difficult problem. Thus tests may be used to develop or evaluate a hypothesis about a baffling problem. In any event, discrimination and judgment are the hallmarks of expertness.

There is no point in reviewing here the great variety of tests for intelligence, aptitude, achievement, and personality available for use, or how to give, score, and interpret them. A recent survey among school psychologists in New York State revealed that the most frequently used individual tests of ability were the Wechsler Intelligence Scale for Children (WISC), and the Stanford-Binet Scales. Commonly used individual tests of personality included the Rorschach test, figure drawing tests, sentence completion tests, the House-Tree-Person Test, the Bender Visual Motor Gestalt Test, and various picture story tests. Numerous books are available, describing in detail these and other instruments used by the psychologist in assessment work.

It is not necessary for teachers to be intimately familiar with the tests which the psychologist uses. It is part of his expertness to select and interpret data and to communicate results in a manner useful to teachers. Certainly if teachers understand the basic principles of test construction, such as validity, reliability, and norms, the communication may proceed at a more sophisticated level, but they do not need to be knowledgeable about the Rorschach to consider the judgments which the psychologist offers as a result of the use of tests.

Almost all the tests which psychologists use permit observations about behavior which in some degree is also observable to the teacher in the classroom situation. Teachers make observations about intelligence, temperament, aptitude, achievement, and personality in the course of working with children. Thus a teacher has certain data, albeit unsystematic, to offer in the collaboration with a psychologist. Her observations are made under conditions and in contexts different from those of the psychologist. The object is not to determine who is correct. It is to obtain a better view of the child by integrating both kinds of data, and sifting and examining them to extract their essence.

Case study.   Some problems referred will of course require very intensive study. The psychologist will leave no stone unturned to develop the most comprehensive picture possible of the pupil's difficulties. Data from all the sources previously mentioned may be needed. Information from school records, classroom observations, interviews with the pupil, teacher, principal, and parents, psychological tests, and samples of classroom work will be assembled for careful analysis and interpretation. This procedure is often called conducting a case study or obtaining a case history.

As he studies his data the psychologist may ask such questions as:

> What kind of person is the pupil?
> What are his difficulties?
> What has been the duration and severity of his problems?
> How are the difficulties revealed? Inwardly, outwardly, or both?
> What influences in his history seem to be related to present difficulties?
> What resources does he have for coping with his problems unaided?
> What is the balance between assets and liabilities?
> What assistance has he had in the past?
> What kinds of assistance are needed now?

Data are used to provide tentative answers to these and other questions. The evaluation may point to the need for additional information. There may be sufficient material at hand to organize a case report for presentation to a case conference, or for discussion with the teacher, as the case may be.

Case Conference

Much of the casework of the school psychologist is carried on with teachers through individual conferences. In the course of assembling information, the psychologist may confer with other teachers, the principal, special service personnel, and parents. He collects and evaluates data and formulates tentative hypotheses as he continues in a one-to-one relationship with the teacher.

There are times, however, when—according to his professional judgment—it is desirable to bring together for a case conference all those persons who can contribute to the understanding of a problem situation and who may have a role in the subsequent remedial program. Case conferences require the valuable time of a number of persons; hence, they cannot be justified as routine procedures. In its most general form the case conference is a problem-solving group, which may have one of several interrelated functions. It may be used for assessment, remedial or teaching functions, separately or in combination with other techniques. In this chapter we are primarily concerned with its diagnostic function.

Usually the psychologist, teacher, and the principal are in best position to judge whether or not a case conference is needed. If a problem is evaluated and resolved through the efforts of the teacher and psychologist, involvement of others seems unnecessary. However, some problems are more complex and involve other staff members such as previous teachers, the school nurse, the remedial reading teacher, or the school physician. On the other hand it may be expected that other staff members can contribute not only new information but bring a special perspective to existing information. In any event, the objective for convening a group is to obtain the best possible understanding of the problem at hand.

The prospect of a conference does not always evoke eager expectations in psychologists or educators. This is especially true if they have not participated in satisfying, effective conferences in the past. Much has been learned in recent years about the characteristics which make for effective conferences.[1]

Purpose. The conference should have a clearly stated goal ac-

---

[1] Readers interested in the improvement of conferences might consult M. B. Miles, *Learning to Work in Groups* (New York: Teachers College, Columbia University, 1959).

ceptable to all participants. If possible, the objective and agenda should be sent to participants in advance so that they can prepare themselves. A teacher may want to bring samples of classroom performance by the pupil under study; the nurse may want to consult her records. An agenda should be flexible and it should be reviewed at the beginning of the meeting so that new items may be added if desired. An agenda, accepted by all, often promotes the self-regulation of participation by members at the conference. It provides a focus, suggests a time limit, and helps members and the leader to keep discussion relevant to the issues at hand.

Leadership. One member of the group should be designated to exercise leadership functions essential to effective problem-solving. One finds the psychologist or the principal in this role most frequently. Essential leader functions include stating objectives, reviewing the agenda, assisting members to make their contributions, keeping the task in focus, clarifying issues and conflicting views that may arise, summarizing findings, helping the group periodically test its progress. Some of these roles may, of course, be assumed by other members of the group.

The important point to keep in mind is that these functions must be essayed by one individual, or the group will be less effective than it might be. One argument for having someone function as leader on a fairly regular basis is that he can develop more and more adequate skills in group leadership.

Recorder. A group will function better if some member keeps a record of the essential issues under discussion. Such a running account permits occasional summaries to help the group determine what ground it has covered and where it is in its problem-solving process.

Process. Effective problem-solving includes a clear definition of the problem to be solved and the procedures for solution. After the problem has been clearly stated, it may be found that the preliminary studies by the psychologist and the reports and contributions by other group members are sufficient for clear understanding of the problem. On the other hand, additional data may be needed. In such an event, responsibility for obtaining the data should be clearly delegated to someone. If the group has all the information needed, it may proceed to develop a strategy for resolving the problem (see Chapter IV).

It has been found to be most instructive for groups to evaluate their own procedures and ways of working. Procedures or behavior of group members may be reviewed to determine how they contribute to or impede effective group work. While such self-evaluation may engender some anxiety at first, in the long run it brings the satisfaction of more efficient problem-solving. Some groups designate one of their members to make rather systematic observations of their procedures with the aim of feeding the information back to assist members to appraise their procedures.

While group problem-solving is not inherently superior to individual effort, in many situations the case conference is an invaluable device with virtues of its own. It is necessarily the case that each member of the school staff learns about a pupil under limited circumstances. The teacher, the nurse, the special teacher, the principal, and others acquire particular perceptions of a pupil based on their contacts with him. Since each staff member also enacts a different role in the total educational enterprise, he is likely to view a pupil with the expectations relevant to his own role. By bringing together and sharing with one another the varied perceptions, beliefs, and conclusions about a pupil which have developed out of their relationships to him, the school staff can hardly help but develop a somewhat more comprehensive picture of the pupil than can one person alone. Pooling of the data makes new hypotheses possible. Different views of the pupil can be appreciated as resulting both from the different contexts in which the pupil is observed by different persons, and from the fact that the pupil in fact may behave differently in various situations. Conflicting views may be resolved through an awareness that two views may not be conflicting but complementary. Members in a case conference are frequently observed to modify their views after receiving additional data from others. Such changes in belief or attitude may occur imperceptibly as the group engages in the process of problem-solving.

A valuable byproduct of group involvement in trying better to understand a pupil is the enhanced morale of the members. A teacher or psychologist may feel discouraged by individual effort only to find new possibilities after joining efforts with others. Everyone may get a lift from a realization that through joint effort the case may not be as hopeless as it appeared at the outset. This outcome cannot be assumed on sentimental grounds, but is a prospect for those who work hard for the welfare of pupils.

Records and Reports

Records. No case need be made here for the importance of pupil records in the ongoing educational enterprise. Cumulative, longitudinal records for pupils are essential to the effective discharge of the school's instructional, guidance, and legal obligations.

The school psychologist is one among many staff members who contribute data to the cumulative record of a pupil as he progresses through school. The purpose of this section is limited to consideration of the psychologist's own records and how he uses them for the welfare of pupils.

The teacher uses her own professional judgment to determine which observations, opinions, and conclusions—among those available to her—should be inserted into the permanent cumulative record. She does not record everything she knows or thinks she knows. The psychologist is in a similar position with respect to cumulative records. As a result of his observations of a pupil and his casework on problems, he eventually reaches a judgment about the information which eventually may become part of the record.

The psychologist also maintains his own records and files, access to which is more limited. His records may include test protocols, reports of conferences with other school personnel and parents, and personal observations. Since these materials may have been obtained in confidence, or may be of a technical nature understandable only to those with appropriate training, they cannot be generally available if the welfare of pupils is to be the governing criterion. If the psychologist is to function in a truly professional manner, bound by a professional code of ethics, his judgment about access to and uses of his records must be respected.

Effective work with individuals requires that they be permitted at times to request that the psychologist receive their information in strict confidence. When this occurs, the psychologist is ethically obligated to protect this confidence. There are times of course when the psychologist will not accept an offer of confidential information.

Although the major functions of the psychologist's files are to promote the best welfare of pupils, they may also serve subsidiary functions. They may prove useful for a more systematic evaluation of the kinds of problems being encountered by staff and referred to him for study. They may permit an examination of the procedures being used to help pupils and staff with an eye to improving them. They provide useful data for continuing professional development of psychologists on the job.

Reports. The major purpose of reports is to transmit information for effective use by others. Effectiveness of communication is the goal. After a study has been completed, the results and recommendations are prepared for a report.

Psychologists are likely to have a strong preference for personal conferences with teachers as a method for communicating the results of a special study. The reasons for this preference are persuasive. In person-to-person discussion, misperceptions can be clarified and resistances to recommendations can be dealt with. The conference can be healthy for the psychologist in that it may compel him to be practical and realistic and to take the teacher's situation into account. He cannot escape so readily into vague generalizations or unrealistic suggestions. The conference provides a firsthand testing ground to determine whether or not the participants are getting across to one another. And they are likely to persist in working together until the problem is resolved.

Conferences and written reports are not mutually exclusive. In any event the psychologist will prepare a report for his permanent records. He may in some situations send a report to a teacher to be followed later by discussion of it. He may, after a conference, prepare a report so that he and the teacher have a record of their combined effort.

Although there are situations in which the written report is the sole method of transmitting results of study and recommendations by the psychologist to the teacher, they must be viewed as second best in view of what we know generally about difficulties of communication even under optimum conditions. Reports should be clear, relevant to questions asked, practical and usable, and above all written with a particular reader in mind. A psychologist's knowledge of the particular teacher's situation, her interests, and her skills is vital if he is to make suggestions which can be implemented.

There are times when the psychologist is called upon to prepare a more technical report for an outside agency or clinic. He prepares quite a different type of report if the intended reader is another professional person in psychology, psychiatry, or social work. When he is authorized by parents to make such a report, the psychologist must be the judge of the content and type of report to be prepared.

Special Services

Principles and methods of assessment have been discussed from the vantage point of the teacher who uses psychological services to further her instructional objectives. However, the services of the school psychologist may be employed on a schoolwide basis as part of the process of evaluation and classification of pupils for special instruction in such areas as mental retardation, reading disability, or high-ability groupings. Although the assessment skills of the psychologist are called upon in the special education programs of most school systems, the precise nature of his role depends upon local circumstances. For example, the availability of a remedial reading specialist may limit his assessment role to the intensive study of individual pupils referred by the specialist. In another situation he may play a much more active part in the evaluation, classification, and program planning for pupils with reading difficulties.

The assessment role of the school psychologist has been considered in terms of general principles and practices assumed to be applicable to a wide variety of specific situations. Flexibility and adaptability are essential, whether the psychologist is serving a particular teacher or meeting a schoolwide need.

CHAPTER IV

Remedial Roles

It was stated previously that inquiries are action-oriented, and are undertaken in the expectation that the difficulties which prompted them may be alleviated or eliminated. Remedial work is the latter phase of a continuous process which begins with a problematic situation and terminates with some kind of solution. Various terms have been used in the literature to describe efforts to change a given situation to a more desirable one, or to help a person modify some aspect of his behavior. They include: remedial work, re-education, rehabilitation, corrective education, counseling, and psychotherapy. In some instances the change focus is on environmental conditions, in others on intrapersonal difficulties, but most frequently involves both the person and the environment external to him. Remedial procedures with individuals and with groups will be considered in this chapter.

Principles and Concepts

It is assumed that all individuals have some capacity for modification of their behavior. This assumption is basic to any educational or remedial enterprise. In fact, it is a fundamental principle of living. Change and adaptation are required as a condition of survival and in fact define growth and development of all living organisms.

The question to be confronted in a practical sense may be something like this. On the basis of our understanding of the present situation, what kinds of changes are needed, reasonable, feasible, or achievable within what limits of time and resources? What lacks have been identified in knowledge, skill, belief, attitude, relationship, or value? What can be done about them? Who shall be involved? What motivation for change has been identified? Facing such practical decisions counteracts common tendencies to frame questions in all-or-none fashion, such as, "What can be done to change personality?" or "He's hopeless, so why make the effort?" or "It's just a stage, so let him live through it."

The view of the writer is that many kinds of change are worth striving for, large or small, short- or long-term, fragmentary or whole. The specific circumstances will govern the type and magnitude of change to be sought. This admittedly pragmatic approach to problem-solving, which seeks to improve conditions in a realistic way, is a widely shared and accepted view in our complex and diversified educational enterprise. Although philosophical discussions of basic educational issues and concern for more radical revision of educational purposes and procedures are always pertinent in our society, immediate problems of pupils are always before us, requiring assessment and solution in the day-to-day life of the schools.

A key concept which relates remedial work to other activities of the school is that of learning. Learning is the accepted business of the school and the central task of the classroom. As a concept, learning may reflect a continuous relationship between ongoing regular classroom activities and those in special service or remedial work. Remedial work differs from regular teaching not in its educational objectives or underlying concepts but in the use of special techniques and skills by specially trained personnel working in contrived situations to solve particular problems. Remedial work as conceived here does not differ remarkably from other activity carried out in the school. Often its effectiveness depends upon the greater amount of teaching skill made available to individuals and small groups than is possible in the usual oversized classroom. It is at least a reasonable hypothesis that if more effective means for individualizing instruction were found, there would be a decline in the need for remedial services of many kinds.

Although the concept of learning has power for unifying sometimes divergent views about different activities in the schools, decisions must nevertheless be made about the kinds and extent of remedial services to be assumed by the schools and those to be handled by other institutions in the community. Controversy may arise about the respective roles of the school and other institutions, if indeed they exist at all in a given locale, with respect to emotional or social disturbances in pupils. In my view, each community must determine for itself how social resources to promote the development of its children and youth shall be deployed among its institutions, including the school. If past experience is a reliable indicator, we may expect decisions to be made not arbitrarily or on the basis of generalized prescriptions but in light of all the factors which a community deems relevant.

As suggested earlier, the particular remedial methods to be employed and their effectiveness are determined to a large extent by the careful delineation of problems during assessment. Although it is usually assumed that something constructive can be accomplished in most cases, it is not assumed that success will crown all efforts. Lack of skill, knowledge, motivation or cooperation will be encountered in some instances. This point may seem obvious but is emphasized here because highly motivated professional workers sometimes expect too much to happen, or expect it to happen quickly. Some problems are refractory in the face of the very best intentions, skill, and knowledge available.

The psychologist plays a major role in developing the remedial plans after assessment. Since a plan almost always involves other school personnel to some extent, he becomes part of a team effort to arrive at procedures believed to have the best chance of success. All resources available within and outside the school are considered and their potential contribution is evaluated. In the largest segment of cases this involves the psychologist and the teacher. If additional resources are needed, however, the nurse, the remedial reading teacher and other teachers, the principal, the speech teacher, or the physician may participate. Delegation of responsibility is made on the basis of functional competence for the task.

In some instances, the psychologist serves as coordinator of the services provided to the child without further direct contact with the pupil. In other cases he may carry the major role in facilitating changes, as through a series of counseling interviews, aimed at correcting distorted perceptions or unfavorable emotional attitudes. Usually the best results are obtained when some level of participation is achieved by all personnel with an immediate stake in the difficulty. For example, the problem may require counseling intervention, remedial work in reading skills, and curricular modifications concurrently. Thus the psychologist, the reading specialist, and the teacher may carry joint responsibility for ameliorative procedures.

Although remedial activity is discussed primarily in terms of services to pupils, educators should be continuously alert for insights about the school program which may result from regular appraisal of remedial programs. The assumption does not have to be made that all needs for services derive from defects in the school program. Some deficits in the learning and development of pupils are certainly more substantially related to defects in the community or, often, in the family. Although educators cannot necessarily reform families and other institutions in the community, there may be occasions when it is desirable, as a function of educational leadership, to remind the commmunity of the responsibilities which the schools are prepared to assume and of problems which are outside the school's present capacity.

Nevertheless schools would do well to keep an eye on remedial activity for cues to deficiencies in quality of teaching, curriculum content, administrative organization and functions, and educational philosophy. The extent of reading difficulties, for example, may point to questions about teaching methods, the quality of teacher performance, or the appropriateness of curriculum material for the ability levels of the pupils involved. The same might be said for extensive problems in the area of mathematics.

On the other hand, a high incidence of emotional difficulties in the early grades may direct attention to the areas of the community from which the pupils come, as well as to their experiences within the school. It also raises questions about the educational philosophy of the school with respect to responsibility for remedial work.

We may safely assume that the day will never arrive when remedial activities will not be needed in human affairs. Despite human aspirations for perfection, all ways of knowing or doing turn out to be imperfect, even though they may be more adequate than the methods they have replaced.

The concept of remedial activity should not be viewed merely in its negative aspects. On the positive side it reflects a recurrent aspiration for greater competence and ever higher levels of excellence in every sphere of life. It offers a second chance when our wisest calculations go awry. It is a necessary complement to every human invention, even as the search for a better one goes on.

Individual Procedures

All remedial procedures are aimed at changing persons or circumstances for the better. For purposes of discussion, it may be useful to consider change-efforts in relation to the focus of change. The
categories below are obviously interrelated and all of them may be
pertinent—to varying degrees—in any individual case. In another
instance, effort may be concentrated primarily or exclusively in one
area.

> Change in the pupil himself.
> Change in the relations of the pupil to other persons.
> Change in other persons who relate to the pupil.
> Change in the situation confronting the pupil.

Change in the pupil himself.   The success of counseling with a
pupil will depend upon the quality of relationship established. If
the counselor is effective in communicating an acceptant attitude,
the pupil will feel free to learn more about the feelings and attitudes
which he holds toward himself and toward others and about the
ways in which he perceives conditions in the world about him. The
pupil may not be expected to take the counselor "on faith." Only
if he *experiences* [or perceives] genuine interest on the part of the
counselor will he be likely to feel free to discuss openly the more
troublesome aspects of his feelings and actions.

A pupil usually approaches a psychologist with some apprehension. He expects something to be done *to* him, rather than real-
izing that counseling is a process in which his active participation
will be required for effective results. Patience and time will be required for the counselor to define the situation in these terms and to
gain the confidence of the pupil.

Although the counselor may state his belief that pupils in general
have capacity for growth toward more mature functioning through
the processes of counseling, he will have doubts in particular instances. Pupils who are defiant, aggressive, hostile, dependent, withdrawn, or overcompliant may challenge his deepest convictions. But
in any given case he will not know whether his assumption is valid
until he has attempted to establish a relationship on some basis.

It is generally assumed that the pupil's perception of himself and
others exerts considerable influence on his behavior. Thus the first

goal may be to help the pupil discover just what his current perceptions are, without subjecting them to evaluation, judgment, or condemnation. As the pupil learns more about himself and his situation, and can recognize his feelings, attitudes, and actions as truly his own, the next step may be to determine whether he desires to modify them in any way in anticipation of more satisfying results.

We may assume that with clearer awareness of his perceptions and behavior, he is likely to conclude that there is room for improvement. Only when he has a clearer perception of reality and a desire to change some aspects of it for the better can meaningful changes in his behavior be expected. After arriving at this point, the counselor and the pupil must consider new courses of action, try them out, and evaluate the consequences. (This capsule view of counseling may appear too simple and abbreviated. The interested reader is urged to consult the many helpful books now available on the subject listed in the Bibliography.)

Younger pupils frequently cannot participate effectively in this kind of verbal interaction. For them, some kind of play situation may be indicated. Play therapy has proved a highly efficacious procedure in enabling some younger children to work out their tensions and problems in a free play situation. Verbal exchange with an adult may be at a minimum, yet children have been observed to achieve more appropriate adjustments through emotion-releasing play and a secure relationship with an accepting adult over a period of time. A special room may be set aside (or a corner of the psychologist's office may be used) and equipped with the materials found through experience to be particularly useful for play therapy. Most children under ten respond favorably to play therapy but methods used in individual cases must be left to the judgment of the psychologist.

In many instances, the goal of play therapy will be to stimulate the emotional growth of the child apart from academic considerations. In other cases psychologists have been successful in combining play therapy with tutorial approaches to the improvement of certain skills (such as reading).

The kind of helping process conceived here cannot take place in busy corridors or on the run between classes. It is essential to have time for development and a place for privacy where the rest of the world can be shut out. It is also essential that information be kept confidential if innermost thoughts and feelings are to be expressed and discussed. There is always the danger that busy counselors will become so preoccupied with the overt symptoms of the pupil that they will try to bring about temporary overt changes rather than deal with the underlying difficulties.

Counseling is not always a smooth process; the understanding and patience of the teacher are essential to the total effort. If she understands and is sympathetic with the goals and processes of counseling, she can be relied upon to reinforce the counselor's efforts through her own attitudes and actions toward the pupil in the classroom. This will happen only when the counselor and teacher work cooperatively.

Counseling may occur on a regularly scheduled basis over varying periods of time. Many problems, however, may be handled adequately in only one or two sessions.

Questions sometimes arise about the utility of working with the individual alone, without the extensive involvement of his parents. Some writers have concluded that little can be accomplished in this manner. Although concurrent counseling may be desirable, there are numerous instances where it cannot be arranged. Other psychologists have reported success in working with individuals alone. The critical factor may be the inner resources which a given pupil possesses for dealing with his problems. Existing research does not provide conclusive evidence on this point and therefore doctrinaire positions must be suspect. Under present circumstances, the decision should be based on an evaluation of all relevant factors in the case.

In instances where the school's resources are limited or inadequate, the pupil may be referred to an outside agency—such as a guidance clinic—or to a private practitioner. Usually the psychologist takes the lead in effecting such arrangements—if possible, by stimulating the parents to action. But, he continues to serve as liaison between the agency and the school community.

Changes in the relations of the pupil to other persons. The relations of a pupil to his peers and to adults are closely related to his self-perceptions. A pupil who perceives himself as inadequate may well act toward others as if he were inadequate. A pupil who has not learned how to make others comfortable will have difficulties in a social situation. A pupil who has acquired a dislike for a teacher may find his attitude affecting his response to the teacher's requests.

It is possible to consider these instances exclusively in terms of self-perceptions the modification of which is a prerequisite to any improvement in relations with others. Such a view argues that better social interactions will occur almost inevitably once the pupil has set his own house in order. It should be stated that there is some empirical evidence to support this view.

Although the difference may be chiefly one of emphasis, another view considers it desirable to focus change efforts directly in the problem area: social interactions. A pupil deficient in social skills may be given guidance in ways of talking with others or placed in a particular group which is sensitive to his needs and willing to help him. A boy may have erroneous ideas about the unfavorable perceptions of him held by others. By providing him with a more accurate picture of the views of others, the counselor may help him approach them with new confidence and expectations. A girl may believe that other girls consider her unattractive. The counselor or teacher, knowing that this is not the case, may lead her to realize the facts of the situation or may encourage others to express their views to her directly. If the real capabilities of a pupil have not been noticed by others, the teacher may assist him to achievements of greater visibility, thus eliciting the admiration of others and placing future relations on a more adequate basis.

Relationships with peers and adults often provide the testing ground for new, hard-won insights about oneself. Awareness that one is potentially a person of worth in the eyes of others must be put to the test by interacting with others in meaningful ways and then evaluating the consequences. Some views about oneself require validation through information from others about their perceptions. If these principles are kept in mind, specific opportunities for application will be suggested as the counselor works with pupils to improve their relations with others.

A pupil may confess a belief that a teacher or another adult perceives him in a particular way. He may complain that he is blamed for everything that goes wrong in class, that the teacher seems only to see his unacceptable behavior. By helping him to review his behavior and encouraging him to experiment with different types of responses, the counselor can help him test whether his perceptions are valid. The pupil might be encouraged to volunteer where he has not done so before, or to greet the teacher in a friendly way. By departing from his typical modes of response, he may find that the teacher notices the difference and a new relationship may develop.

Sociometric devices have proved useful for obtaining systematic information about the perceptions which pupils have of one another. The teacher is in best position to obtain the data by asking questions suited to the circumstances in her class, such as "Whom would you like to sit next to?" or "Whom would you invite to a party?" The information can be charted, thus giving a picture of the social preferences within the group. Or the "Guess Who" technique might be employed by describing a role characteristic of the age group and asking pupils to name classmates who fit the description. Although the data derived from these devices may be used for various instructional purposes, our interest here is in the information made available about the particular pupil whom the counselor is trying to help. It may result, for example, that a pupil is given favorable ratings by several members of the class, even while he protests that no one likes him. On the other hand, he may express preferences for certain pupils who do not "choose" him. The information may be used either in counseling or through working with the teacher in the classroom to create an interpersonal situation in which old attitudes may be modified.

Changes in other persons who relate to the pupil. Intervention to improve the behavior of a pupil frequently takes the form of seeking to change the perceptions and behavior of adults and peers who stand in a significant relation to him. Other persons behave toward the pupil in accordance with their views of him. For instance, a teacher may become quite annoyed by the antics of a troubled youngster who seems bent on disrupting the class. She may have little information which would suggest reasonable hypotheses about the sources of his behavior. Since the pupil's behavior is not understandable on the basis of available information, she is annoyed and unsympathetic. But after the psychologist, on the basis of individual study, has a chance to talk with the teacher and provide information about the boy's extremely insecure home situation, his fear of rejection by her, and his lack of skill in satisfying certain needs, the teacher may find her attitude toward the boy undergoing change. She may come to feel sympathy instead of annoyance. She recognizes that his behavior in disrupting the class cannot be justified, yet her new attitude toward him leads her to approach him in a friendly rather than a hostile way. He may come to respond favorably and his misbehavior may diminish. Changes such as this do not occur without effort but they do occur frequently.

It is a remarkable fact that when we view the world through the eyes of another person, his behavior often appears more reasonable than when we view his behavior through our own eyes. When we view his behavior as following from his particular way of construing things, the whole sequence makes more sense, even if we cannot approve of the behavior. Such appreciation moves us toward compassion rather than intolerance, toward understanding rather than condemnation.

In working with others who have reached an impasse in their relations with the pupil, the counselor can do nothing more significant and hopeful of bettering relations than to encourage them to imagine how he is perceiving the world, including them. This effort takes them away from defending their present unproductive perceptions and directs their attention to the ever-fascinating challenge of trying to understand another person.

The behavior of another person, which may baffle us at first, may be quite comprehensible when we understand its antecedents. The teacher who views the pupil's sleepy behavior as a threat to her stimulus value as a teacher may take quite a different attitude when she learns that his sleep is disturbed by family quarrels. Much of the psychologist's assistance to teachers consists of efforts to identify antecedent events in the life of the pupil which will "explain" present behavior.

The concepts which have been discussed above are also pertinent in working with parents. In working with parents, the goal of the psychologist is often to help them achieve a more realistic understanding and comprehensive view of their child's needs and the conditions required to meet them. As the parent and psychologist share their observations about a child, a more inclusive picture of the child may emerge. Often the picture, which is broader in perspective, suggests cues for new actions which are absent in the more limited view.

The focus of discussion may well be the home and how the parents may supplement and reinforce the remedial approach in the school. It may include some very specific things for the parents to do, or it may be a more general encouragement of the efforts of the school. In any event, the psychologist may engender an attitude of hope where parents felt apathetic or hopeless. This is often the most important single factor in the improvement of a situation.

Sometimes the goal is to facilitate changes among peers to create a more favorable interpersonal situation for the pupil. Peers, like teachers, may develop fixed, categorical ideas about a pupil that standardize their reactions to him. Procedures may take the form of encouraging peers to include the pupil in their activities or helping teachers to study the social structure of the class for suggestions as to which group might be most receptive. Even general class discussion about individual behavior may help pupils appreciate the fact that they may be unduly intolerant of each other's peculiarities.

Changes in the situation confronting the pupil. The discussion thus far has stressed the importance of changes within the pupil and in his relations with others and changes in the persons who play a significant role in his interpersonal environment. Since behavior is being viewed as a function of the interaction of the pupil with external realities, attention should be given to emphases in remedial work which involve changes in the external environment. Illustrations might include modifications of the curriculum, tutorial assistance in skill areas, changes in class placement, and changes in the home environment through guidance of parents.

As a result of his study, the psychologist may work with the teacher to effect changes in work expectations within the classroom situation. During a period of emotional stress, the work load may have to be reduced while other assistance is being rendered. The current learning expectancies may be beyond the functioning capacity of the pupil. On the other hand, the expectancies may be too low for the pupil's talents and the curriculum may have to be made more challenging. An appropriate balance between capacity and expectation may have desirable therapeutic consequences. In any event, the adjustments made should be viewed as experimental so that revisions may be made as indicated by the results.

In other situations, a significant deficiency may have been identified in reading or arithmetic and tutorial assistance may appear to be desirable. Whether it is conducted by the classroom teacher or a specialist outside the classroom depends, of course, on the special circumstances in the school. If reading or speech help is given outside the classroom, it is important that it be integrated with the classroom situation.

There are times when the persons formulating a remedial program will judge that a different class placement is indicated. It may take the form of placement in a special class, or of assignment to a more appropriate teacher. Such changes are not made without the most careful review of alternative courses of action. In larger cities, a change to a school specializing in particular functions may be possible.

In some instances, the very best adjustments that the school can make may prove to be ineffective without changes in the home environment. By working with parents, effort may be directed to provide a more favorable study environment in the home, to lighten the burden of family chores being imposed on the pupil, and to encourage the parents to provide more support of the pupil's learning efforts. Whatever their own difficulties and problems, most parents respond favorably to the efforts of the school to adapt its procedures to help their child and this very demonstration of interest makes them receptive to potential remedial efforts in the home.

If parents are unable or unwilling to cooperate, school personnel will have to rely upon their own resources. A genuine attempt to help, even when accompanied by doubts, may communicate a sense of hope to a pupil who feels that nobody really cares and that his situation is completely hopeless. Many experienced psychologists and teachers report such occurrences although they had not predicted them.

Group Procedures

The school psychologist does not rely solely upon working with individuals; he is also alert to the change-possibilities inherent in groups. The basis for this view is not merely economy of time but the recognition that there is considerable evidence that groups can exert great influence in changing the behavior of individual members. In recent years substantial progress has been made in understanding of group behavior and in developing practical means for using forces in group life for purposes of instruction, guidance, counseling, and psychotherapy. It is not our purpose to review the growing literature in this area, but to suggest some of the uses of groups for remedial work.

The class as a group.   Some writers have referred to the classroom as a miniature society, or a subcultural group, with an identity of its own—with norms, expectations, and systems of reward and punishment, which cannot be understood in terms of the individuals who are members. Teachers have been heard to say, "My class this year has a different personality from the one I had last year," or "I have a wonderful class this year." Obviously the reference is in some sense to a group rather than to an aggregation of individuals. As more is learned about group behavior, teachers and psychologists have become sensitive to possibilities for manipulating forces in groups to enhance normal development as well as to provide clues for assisting youngsters in need of help.

One of the reasons the psychologist may observe a pupil in the classroom situation is that he gains an impression of the emotional climate in the group, an awareness of how a given pupil is reacted to by others, and some picture of how the pupil relates to others. Such observations may not only assist in an assessment of difficulties but also provide suggestions for ways in which changes in the group might assist the pupil to better adjustment. For example, if it appears that the problem pupil admires one of the class leaders, the possibility of later involving the admired leader in some phase of the remedial program may be considered.

The teacher may use sociometric devices for studying the social structure of the class. Although currently operating cliques or subgroups may be identified by these procedures, the data are best viewed as sources of hypotheses about the underlying forces in the classroom, for they reveal little about why these groups exist or the bases on which they were formed. Additional inquiries are needed, perhaps about the socio-economic status of parents, neighborhood gangs, clubs, or community organizations. Classroom observations of participation patterns during discussions or of spontaneous groupings during free play periods may provide further insights. The enterprising teacher might also study the relationship of different groupings to various kinds of school achievement, aptitudes, abilities, interests, or attitudes toward particular facets of school life.

The data collected from various sources may provide clues to dealing with disciplinary difficulties, to understanding motivations toward achievement, or to solving other problems of classroom management. Too frequently, issues about discipline or achievement motivation are considered primarily in terms of the individual characteristics of the pupil or of the teacher's skill and experience, without taking into account the social forces in the classroom. Working together, the teacher and the psychologist may find some of the approaches suggested here productive of new opportunities for enhancing the development of pupils as well as for initiating corrective action when problems arise.

One sixth-grade teacher had been having considerable difficulty with several boys in her class. She observed that when one "acts up" in class, several other boys tended to support his unacceptable behavior. She mentioned her concern one day in an informal discussion with the school psychologist. He became interested and they decided to see whether they could determine what was going on. The teacher gave a sociometric test and on analysis they discovered that four boys constituted a group whose members chose one another to the exclusion of all other members of the class. They also discovered that no other member of the class selected any of the four boys. Then they searched for information as to whether or not the four boys shared other characteristics in common. The records disclosed that the four were in the bottom fourth of the class in achievement although they were about at the class median in intelligence. Informal inquiries made to other students revealed that the boys spent a great deal of time together outside of school and came from families with similar socio-economic backgrounds. They also learned that the boys were not unpopular, nor were they popular; they were simply ignored. These conversations with other members of the class revealed a note of superiority: the four boys were from a less attractive part of town and were unlikely to go to college. Since the school was in one of the better suburban areas where most of the pupils were college-bound, the curriculum was strongly oriented toward academic studies.

By now the hypothesis was emerging from the data at hand that the group banded together for mutual support and defense and could gain recognition only through creating disturbances in class. It appeared to the teacher and psychologist that they had to do something to break through the social class lines that had been drawn. Although the boys had reasonable academic ability, they shared negative attitudes toward school. But the problem in the classroom seemed to be the rejection of the small group by the rest of the class.

Several approaches were tried. The teacher made a special effort to get better acquainted with each of the boys individually. They responded to her new interest in them. As she learned more about them, she found her attitude becoming more sympathetic and less impatient. During a social studies unit on the community, the psychologist was invited to visit the class and lead a discussion on the ways that different value systems in the home affected attitudes toward social institutions and how these attitudes were expressed in personality development. The class became deeply interested and several more sessions were held on the topic. By skillful handling of the subject, the psychologist was able to elicit the points of view, prejudices, and values of members of the class. The value of respecting differences was highlighted. Although the discussion became heated at times, it was brought to a successful conclusion with general acceptance of the idea that differences may enrich life rather than be divisive. During the discussions it was noted that the four boys were very much involved, and their views were accorded due respect.

Two weeks later, another sociometric test was administered and the four boys were no longer isolated from the rest of the class. The teacher had also observed in the interim that the boys were showing greater interest in the class and were no longer creating disturbances.

Not all difficulties in a class will yield to these approaches: the point to be emphasized is not the particular techniques used but the concept behind them. The assumption was made that a scrutiny of the total class situation was required rather than intensive individual studies of the four boys. Thus behavior may be more fruitfully understood in terms of a larger social system than some traditional clinical viewpoints might suggest. It should be noted also that the remedial approach concentrated on the entire group in order to upset existing channels of interaction and to create new ones in their place.

Remedial groups. It is common practice in schools to group pupils who have a similar difficulty, such as a reading deficiency. Careful appraisal through use of one of the many fine diagnostic reading surveys available should precede assignment to such a group. The size of the group cannot readily be specified, for such factors as the skill of the teacher, the goals and duration of the group, the frequency of meetings, and the severity of the difficulties will have a significant bearing on results that may be anticipated. If a group is composed of pupils with reasonably similar difficulties, some of the instruction can be directed to the group as a whole even though individual tutoring will also be necessary. As the disabilities in the group become more heterogeneous, more individualized attention will be required. This factor alone will influence the size of the group that can be handled efficiently within a given period of time.

It is often claimed that remedial reading groups are used as "dumping grounds" for academic failures which arise from a variety of problems, such as emotional disturbances, social and cultural deprivation, and unconcealed hostility to the purposes and values of the school. Although pupils with these difficulties require assistance, little is gained by placing them with reasonably motivated pupils whose problem is a reading deficiency. In fact they will not only fail to profit from the experience but will become a deterrent to the learning of others in the group.

Reading authorities do not prescribe a standard approach to remedial groups. Flexibility in procedures based upon a clear picture of the needs of the members is indicated. The teacher must be sensitive to the emotional dimensions of the group, for it is probable that anxiety, fear of failure, and impaired self-esteem will be found among most of its members. Even where the chief objective is the improvement of specific reading skills, time may be given to dealing with emotional and social needs. If an emotional climate which is experienced by pupils as hopeful and optimistic can be developed, the prospects for desirable outcomes will be greatly enhanced.

No matter what criteria for acceptance into the group are employed, individual differences in attitude, interest, and effort may be expected. Thus the procedures will include work with the group as a whole, with subgroups, and with individuals. Trained remedial specialists usually work with the groups although it is not unknown for the school psychologist competent in this area to work with one or more groups. More frequently, however, he may serve as a consultant to the teacher, helping where he can by making more intensive individual studies on referral or by discussing remedial procedures and assisting in the evaluation of outcomes.

The school psychologist may play an important part in helping to identify a school's need for remedial services and to establish such programs. As he works with individual pupils, he may become aware of the extent to which particular academic deficiencies exist in a given school. By talking with teachers, he may come to learn of common difficulties among pupils. If there is a schoolwide testing program, he may study the records available on the total pupil population or on selected segments of it. As he examines the relationships between ability and achievement, he may discover areas of difficulty in mathematics or other subjects for which good reading skills are necessary. He may suggest that a reading survey or tests of basic study skills be carried out to provide a more comprehensive factual basis for determining needs. The value of systematic surveys over more informal approaches is in the assurance that the needs of all pupils will be reviewed.

Counseling and therapy groups.   Groups are sometimes formed where the avowed purpose is not specifically instructional but to help members work on their social and emotional difficulties. They may meet on a regular basis during the school day with a specially trained leader—perhaps the psychologist himself. It makes no functional difference whether such groups are designated as guidance, counseling, or therapeutic groups. Local customs and preferences will govern the designation. The use of such groups has been increasing and the interest is greater than it has ever been.

There are many reasons for this development. The most important justification is its promise for helping troubled youngsters to improve their capabilities for making maximum use of the educational opportunities afforded by the school. Emotional and social difficulties have been shown to be detrimental to intellectual development. Often the difficulties of a pupil cannot be effectively dealt with in the regular classroom, or the resources for individual assistance may be severely limited. The more persuasive reasons for group approaches to particular problems lie, however, within the potentialities of groups to influence particular individuals toward more adequate modes of behavior.

Some values distinctive to guidance groups may be suggested briefly, even at the risk of oversimplification:

1. A situation is provided in which the pupil may observe first-hand how others perceive and act toward him. One effect of anxiety is to dull the discrimination of differences in the attitudes of others. "Everyone is against me," or "Nobody understands or cares about me," illustrate the all-or-none character of perceptions under conditions of extreme anxiety or fear. Interchange of ideas and feelings in a group in which anxieties and fears have been reduced may gradually lead to a sharpened awareness that attitudes are held in varying degrees of intensity and may differ widely among members of the group. Clarity in perception of the real differences in attitudes may lead to more realistic and constructive action.

2. The pupil has a chance to evaluate how he feels and acts toward others. He may acquire hostile feelings toward particular persons who have treated him unfairly, but he soon projects or displaces his feelings to others so that he may come to feel more or less hostile toward all other persons. He may deny feeling hostile even as he acts in a hostile way. Under sensitive leadership in a group, he may be led to appreciate the pervasiveness of his distorted perceptions and be helped to see others more realistically.

3. The recognition that others have similar anxieties, fears, and problems can be reassuring. A commonly reported outcome of participation in therapy groups is the comforting awareness that one is not alone in being afraid or in feeling unworthy or hostile. Anxiety tends to separate people from one another, thus intensifying the anxiety that normally attends "aloneness." Although it is true that sharing a "common fate" with others may not dissipate the undesired emotions, each may feel strengthened to face his own problems when others are perceived as facing similar problems.

4. The willingness of others to discuss their difficulties openly may be encouraging to the more reserved, or frightened pupil. Frequently it is extremely difficult for a pupil to unburden himself to an adult in individual sessions. Even the highly permissive counselor finds that long-established habits of difficulty in relating to adults are not easily overcome in some pupils. Yet with peers who find it easier to talk about themselves, such pupils will gradually bring out their own concerns and problems.

5. Despite their own difficulties, pupils often contribute valuable suggestions to others about ways to cope with their problems. The therapeutic potential in groups, apart from the skill and wisdom of the leader, has often been noted by writers in the field. No matter how well-intentioned and highly skilled the leader may be, he is likely to be out of touch with some facets of the peer culture. A wise counselor will allow ample opportunity for members of the group to help one another.

6. The emotional support which members can give to one an-

other is a potent factor in promoting change in behavior. Although members of a group may feel hostile and verbally attack each other, compassion does break through eventually and exerts a powerful healing influence. A desire to help others is often hidden from view by the more visible defenses of hostility, anger, and aggressiveness. As a group progresses and these defenses become less necessary, more positive, affiliative tendencies appear.

The extent to which these values may be realized depends chiefly upon the quality of leadership. Good intentions and a few courses are not sufficient. Sound training under supervision as well as personal qualities are essential. As more school psychologists become aware of the possibilities inherent in group therapy for helping troubled youngsters, they are obtaining additional training to use these techniques. Very few psychologists have had such training prior to entry into the field.

Although the use of therapy groups in the schools is not widespread at the present time, interest in this approach is growing. Because experience has been limited, general answers to likely questions cannot be given. What kinds of problems can best be handled by these methods? What criteria shall be used for selection of pupils? What is the optimum size of a group? How frequently and over how long a period shall such groups meet? How shall coordination with regular classes be maintained? What will be the probable reactions of other school personnel if such a program is started?

Reports in the literature about the exploratory use of groups in different situations indicate that these questions have been given serious attention and have been answered in terms of local circumstances. Some of the answers reflect adaptations of experience with groups in other types of institutions. For example, the view that a group functions best with six to ten members has been found generally applicable. On the other hand, the expectation that groups meet from one-and-a-half to two hours has not been found readily adaptable to the school schedule of one-hour periods, unless the activity is carried on after school hours. In general, it may be said that schools interested in experimental work in this area have found it best to rely upon the leadership role of the school psychologist for dealing with relevant issues. In this writer's view, greater use of group therapy techniques may be expected in the future.

Groups as social inventions. The formation of remedial groups within the structure of school society may engender unexpected problems. They may be perceived as a panacea for all difficulties. Overburdened teachers may assign troublesome pupils to such groups in order to gain relief from harassment in the regular classroom. The principal or teachers may view the existence of ameliorative groups as visible evidence of failure in the regular instructional program. The groups may become the dumping ground for all pupils who are not able to keep pace with their peers. Thus a leader may be faced with a heterogeneous collection of pupils whose common symptom is unfitness for school society.

Such situations are not likely to occur if attention is given to the dynamics of social invention. Almost any change in an ongoing situation may be seen as threatening and disturbing if the persons affected by the change are not involved in the process. This principle suggests that when remedial groups are to be introduced, processes of consultation by leadership with school staff should be instituted to prepare for the change. If possible, discussions by the entire staff concerning needs for such groups, purposes to be sought, effects of new procedures on old practices, and other issues should be fully discussed. Ideally, the actual changes should be the result of consensus among all concerned even though particular persons assume major responsibilities for execution of different phases of the plan. It is also desirable that continuing evaluation of the innovation be provided for.

CHAPTER V

Consultant Roles

Thus far we have considered the school psychologist in his more traditional assessment and remedial roles. Field studies have indicated that in most school systems he devotes a major part of his working day to the fulfillment of these functions. In many places, however, his functions are being expanded and made available to the entire pupil population and to other school personnel. In his newer roles, he is often referred to as a "mental health consultant" or, simply, "consultant."

Working with Teachers

The school psychologist's effectiveness is reflected through his success in working with teachers. In assisting the teacher to provide an optimum learning environment for each pupil, he brings psychological knowledge, understanding, and skill to bear upon this fundamental mission of the school. His relations with teachers become the media through which psychological science and practice contribute to the growth and development of pupils.

Despite a common purpose, conflicts do arise between psychologists and teachers. Differences in training, task orientation and perception, personal goals, and cultural stereotypes may generate difficulties in relationships and in communication. The extensive individual differences among psychologists and teachers make general statements about each group somewhat precarious but worth consideration by thoughtful readers.

The psychologist. The psychologist in the school is likely to show a considerable interest in particular children, especially those about whom questions have been raised by the staff. When problems are referred to him, he becomes concerned about the source of current behavior, what it means, and where it is headed. This "clinical" interest may be perceived as preoccupation with deviation or pathology, or as identification with the welfare of a few pupils without regard to the larger population or the essential task of the school.

This orientation is at least a partial result of the psychologist's training and the way he views his task. Although the view taken here argues for a much broader function for the psychologist, it does not diminish the importance of his role in working intensively with individual pupils who need help. The training of the psychologist is individual-centered in its clinical aspects. Theories and diagnostic and remedial methods tend to emphasize the individual rather than the group.

Of great importance to the success of the consultant role is the psychologist's own image of himself. If he views every problem as requiring protracted investigation and extensive rehabilitation, he will lose numerous opportunities to assist in the solution of many problems for which psychological principles and techniques are available for application. Consultation is often more difficult than lengthier procedures, for it requires great flexibility in mobilizing resources of knowledge and skill to meet the requirements of problems in which time does not permit extensive consideration.

Some psychologists have previously taught in the public schools and may therefore have a more sophisticated appreciation of the teaching function than those with other backgrounds. When such a person changes professions, however, he is likely to take on the cultural coloration of the newer profession. In any event, there is no substantial evidence that psychologists with teaching experience work more effectively with teachers than those without such experience. Although some educators assume that teachers make better school psychologists, this issue should be subjected to research rather than argument.

Psychologists are not immune from culture-based attitudes toward the teaching profession. Some of them may share the feeling of low esteem toward teaching which is held by some segments of our society. Even when psychologists rationally accept the worth of teaching as a profession, their dormant prejudices may be evoked by particular teachers and may interfere with the development of desirable relationships.

The teacher. It is a fact of school life that the teacher performs almost all her tasks in a group situation. Although urged to individualize learning and instruction, she has to do it in a class of twenty-five to thirty pupils. Her training and the continuing demands of each day lead her to focus on the present behavior and functions of pupils. Her perceptions are not likely to be oriented toward the past or future during the regular performance of her duties.

Thus the psychologist, with his concern for the individual, may not appreciate that the teacher is viewing the child from a stance that is valid for its purpose, and may perceive her as not "causally" oriented, or as superficial in approach to the understanding of behavior.

The task of providing optimum learning for each child is complex and demanding, if not impossible, under present-day circumstances. Yet the conscientious teacher may blame herself when the goal is not reached in a particular instance. She may construe a request for assistance as a sign of failure on her part. Even when she realizes that factors in the pupil's earlier history at home, in the community, or in the school significantly affect present behavior, she may be reluctant to seek help.

The teacher may, unwittingly or not, share community attitudes toward the mental health professions, including psychology. Her apprehension may lead her to overemphasize the "magical" powers of psychology for clairvoyant diagnosis and cure. She may feel unrealistically guilty about her contribution to the child's problems, and be fearful of disclosing such feelings to another person.

Consultative relationships. Citation of a few potential barriers to good relationships presents the negative side of the situation. Excellent relationships can be developed if they are valued and sought by the participants. The goal is to achieve the kind of communication that is informal, meaningful, and free from threats and fears. It cannot be accomplished without patience, effort, and time.

It may be useful to suggest some of the characteristics of good working relationships. Starting with a conception of their common goal, the teacher and the psychologist must learn what each can and is willing to contribute to the task at hand. There is recognition that each represents a different profession with special knowledge and skills to offer. The relationship is perceived not as that of expert and client, but as that of colleagues joining their efforts to solve problems.

In addition to acknowledging special skills and strengths, each person can admit limitations in knowledge, insight, and skill. If the problems are to be solved, time must not be given to pretension or evasion, but devoted to a joint search for solutions. It is easier for the psychologist to succumb to impulses toward grandiosity, for it is the teacher who first brings the problem to him. Many psychologists have found, however, that their own understanding of a pupil has been greatly enhanced when they sought the help of the teacher. Such recognition of interdependency is a powerful ingredient of mutually satisfactory human relationships.

Consultation, as used in this chapter, refers to the more or less informal, short-term contacts between the psychologist and the teacher about some problem situation. In the long run, consultations are likely to be most effective if they occur within the context of an already established professional relationship. They may then be perceived as brief encounters within a continuing helping relationship. Privacy and time are essential. The psychologist also must maintain flexibility in his schedule so that he may be available when needed without undue delay. Emergencies occur which cannot be placed on a waiting list!

Although the best results are possible only within a relationship which has grown, every relationship must have a beginning. The problems which teachers may bring for consultative assistance may be endless in variety. Questions about the behavior of particular pupils are among the most common. Concerns about more general issues may take the form of asking for help on technical problems about classroom tests, discipline, learning differences among pupils, methods of studying children, interpretation of data in the cumulative record, uses of results of standardized tests, and a host of other issues about which the psychologist may be presumed to have some competence.

Help may take many forms: assisting the teacher to clarify her thinking and feeling about a particular issue, providing technical information or interpretations, suggesting sources of information for further study, or referring the teacher to a more appropriate source of assistance. In these instances, the psychologist is likely to act in an advisory capacity. He does not "take over" the teacher's problems or even participate directly in their solution. His major goal is to enhance the teacher's efforts in problem-solving.

The problem may be in the nature of a crisis. The teacher may have struggled with the problem of a pupil until she is exhausted and sees no way out. She may feel desperate and hopeless about the deadlock which has developed. She obviously needs strong emotional support as well as practical suggestions about what to do. The psychologist must recognize the emergency character of the teacher's feelings and give time even at the cost of revising his schedule.

Although the psychologist should make it possible for the teacher to release her overload of tension, he must keep the focus of discussion on the problem at hand. If he does this skillfully, hopefully, and calmly, he provides the atmosphere for a clearer delineation of the difficulty and communicates the attitude that processes of problem-solving are under way. He does not offer to take over the problem, but may make suggestions which may give new perspective to the problem. In some instances no more is required; in other cases several consultations may be held.

When there is no urgency, consultation proceeds at a more casual pace. Let us assume that a teacher wishes to improve the evaluation procedures used in her classroom. The psychologist might hold series of conferences to help her clarify instructional objectives and define them in measurable terms. They may discuss alternative ways of measurement and the desirable characteristics (such as validity and reliability) of devices. This type of consultation may not be offered as a substitute for a course in measurement, but as a guide for the teacher in her program of self-study. A large amount of the psychologist's time may not be invested in the procedure; he may be involved only at those times when his technical knowledge can be most useful. If a number of teachers acknowledge a similar need, it may be more economical to work on a group basis by establishing an in-service training program (see Chapter VI).

Consultations with teachers about the adjustment of particular pupils are no doubt one of the more frequent activities of school psychologists. Discussions about technical problems occur less often —either because there appears to be less time for them or because the possibilities for obtaining assistance from the psychologists have not yet been discovered. Many of these problems may be perceived as more within the province of the educational psychologist, but until greater specialization occurs within psychology in the schools, they are likely to be referred to the school psychologist.

Group consultation and guidance.   In some school systems, the consultant role of the psychologist has been extended beyond a consideration of fairly specific problems to an exploratory type of counseling or therapeutic activity with teachers. In these instances goals are not usually stated in terms of a focus on basic personality change but on providing teachers with an opportunity to examine the more personal side of the teaching function.

Teaching is recognized as an occupation which makes substantial emotional demands. Working intensively with youngsters of any age generates tensions, anxieties, and feelings of guilt even in the most stable personalities. As the goals of education have enlarged to include concern for the emotional and social dimensions of pupil growth, many problems of great complexity arise for which many teachers have had little or no training. Many experts concerned with mental health in the schools believe that opportunities to discuss such problems can be productive of healthier and more effective teachers. Hence an opportunity may be provided on a voluntary basis for teachers to meet informally with the psychologist, usually in a group situation, to discuss openly their feelings about their work, emotional problems generated by particular pupils, ways in which they respond to pupils, and any other issues which concern them.

The role of the psychologist is typically to listen attentively, to accept and clarify feelings and attitudes, to encourage group members to look as frankly as they can at the difficulties encountered in teaching and their methods of coping with them. He may also make comments and interpretations to facilitate self-understanding and to suggest ways in which teachers may better cope with emotional problems in the classroom. He respects the integrity of the teacher as an expert in her own right but uses his own skill and insight as something of an expert in interpersonal relations to help the teacher better understand the interplay of emotional forces between her and her pupils.

In one instance a teacher remarked that she had particular difficulty in dealing with aggressive boys who habitually flaunted her authority in the class. Other teachers in the group commented that they too had such difficulties. One by one they reported how they felt in such situations, and it was not surprising that different reactions were reported. One felt that she might lose the respect of the class, another reported that she felt angry, while a third mentioned that she merely felt anxious. All of them recalled what they did when they experienced such feelings, and began to see that there was a relationship between their feelings and their behavior.

Gradually the group was able to accept these feelings as valid, even if not particularly noble, and to recognize that their responses to the boys occurred prior to any rational analysis of the situation. They also saw that when their overt actions directly followed their feelings, they were merely contributing to an unproductive sequence of events. Then a common problem was identified: How might such situations be handled more effectively, regardless of different feelings, with presumptively different origins?

The discussion then turned to the reasons why the boys might have been acting aggressively. The teachers as a group tended to feel that they must have done something to evoke, if not cause, the reactions of the boys. The psychologist then focused the concern of the group on the possible reasons for aggression in the particular boys in question. Many possibilities were suggested, including some that had nothing whatever to do with the classroom.

It became apparent that many boys might react to a teacher in a way that should be construed as a reaction toward her not as a person but as a representative of adult authority. Others might be responding to internal tensions which they were unable to control. As the teachers recalled their own experience, they concluded that they had perceived the boys' reactions as a personal affront. This brought out the idea that they might be in a better position to handle situations if they could be somewhat more objective about aggressive actions, rather than respond overtly in purely personal terms.

Ways of achieving such a stance were explored. Some of these ways were getting to know the boys better as persons, asking themselves—when faced with provoking behavior—"What does this mean?" and calmly suggesting to the boy that they might talk things over later. The important point seemed to be that instead of acting directly to retaliate against the boys in terms of personal feelings, a more objective perspective might be achieved by reflecting on what was going on. Later these teachers experimented with different responses and reported increasing competence in handling problems of aggressiveness in class.

It is not intended by this illustration to show how miracles are wrought but to suggest that this kind of consultation is worthy of continuing exploration.

Working with Administrators and Other
Specialized Personnel

Many of the same characteristics and problems about consultative relationships discussed in relation to the psychologist and the teacher are applicable to the relationships between the psychologist and other personnel. Knowledge about and respect for the professional functions of other personnel is an indispensable requirement. Here, too, the psychologist is obliged to identify and interpret the ways in which he may be of assistance.

Administrators. The psychologist must be knowledgeable about the educational and legal functions of the administrator's role. He must also be aware of the ways in which particular administrators discharge their functions. Failure to understand may lead to embarrassment and possible friction and conflict. The knowledge will also be of help as he seeks to define his own role and obligations vis-à-vis administration. Most psychologists recognize that they usually function in a staff rather than line relationship, but sometimes the implications of such a relationship are not fully appreciated.

Personnel functions are generally located in the administrative office. Although a particular school psychologist may possess considerable knowledge about personnel psychology, his roles in this area require thoughtful consideration in relation to his roles in other areas, such as consultation with teachers. The administration may seek his advice about general policies and techniques for screening and evaluating prospective applicants. But if the psychologist is asked to participate in interviewing and making decisions about employment of applicants for teaching positions, he must carefully consider the implications for his other role of maintaining confidential consultative relationships with teachers.

Suppose the psychologist is asked to recommend whether or not a teacher should be reassigned because of ineffectiveness in her current grade placement. He must first see clearly his own role, and then ask whether involvement in this kind of decision will prove detrimental to or inconsistent with his present relationships with teachers. Although it is usually possible to discern the difference between making a decision—obviously the administrator's responsibility—and making a recommendation, the psychologist must be sensitive as to whether or not others perceive such a distinction.

Delicate issues may also arise with respect to the regular evaluations of teachers by administrators. Because he works closely with teachers, the psychologist may have an unusual opportunity to observe their strengths and limitations. But his recognized role is to help teachers, to support and aid in their growth within a process that requires mutual trust and confidence. He may, therefore, decline an offer to participate in merit ratings of particular teachers. The psychologist may be most happy, however, to participate and contribute his expert knowledge to general discussions about the values of merit rating, and alternative techniques of assessment.

The kinds of problems for which the administrator might seek the assistance of the psychologist are quite varied. A few of them will be mentioned and discussed briefly. Maintenance and enhancement of good staff relations and morale are ongoing responsibilities of the administrator. Since he and the psychologist function in different roles, they are likely to see aspects of staff relations and teacher morale from viewpoints that are not only different but complementary. Each may acquire an enriched perspective from an exchange of ideas. If trouble spots occur, they can discuss how to deal with them. The problem may be the particular difficulty of one teacher with classroom discipline, or the competitive relationship between two teachers, or an issue of schoolwide importance such as public criticism of the school which is affecting the morale of the entire staff. The steps to be taken will in each case depend upon an appraisal of the situation. More information may be needed and other staff members may have to become involved before a strategy for corrective action can be initiated.

Problems in the grouping of pupils for instruction are recurrent issues in the life of the school. The psychologist may be asked to present to the staff the current theoretical issues and research findings. He may help to study the effects of present grouping and evaluate need for revision. Criteria for new grouping will be established, after which he may help determine the measures needed to meet these standards. Plans for the periodic evaluation of new programs should be formulated as an integral part of the process of revision.

Administrators recognize the importance of interpreting the school program to the community as a regular responsibility. The basis for consultation may be how best to present information to achieve the greatest educative and public relations impact. The content may be the reading program, pupil personnel services, or the science program in the intermediate grades. Of course, other staff members will be involved, but the psychologist's knowledge about planning meetings for large or small groups or evaluating the effects of the presentation may be especially useful. Effective public information programs have the merit of reducing or preventing irresponsible and uninformed criticism of the school. When such criticisms do arise, a way for analyzing and coping with them must be devised. The extent and sources of the criticism must be appraised prior to developing a counteracting strategy. If the school psychologist has had training in social psychology, he can be very helpful in dealing with such problems.

It is not assumed that every school psychologist can be helpful for every type of problem that has a psychological dimension. He is, after all, not a superman. Moreover, it is incumbent upon the psychologist to know his own capabilities and to inform administrators about the areas in which he might be of assistance. On the other hand, as administrators recognize the potential contributions of psychology to education, they are more likely to seek assistance. If the services desired are beyond the capacity of present staff or the time available to it, a basis exists for seeking additional persons on a full-time, part-time, or independent consultant basis.

Consultation is frequently requested on matters of curriculum development and improvement. Many schools have regular or ad hoc committees on curriculum with which the psychologist is asked to serve in a consultant capacity. These requests are quite appropriate, for most issues in planning, revising, or evaluating programs of study have psychological dimensions. Developmental characteristics of pupils at various age levels, problems of learning and motivation in relation to the content of subjects, questions about grade placement of materials, and evaluation of programs are among the recurrent issues in curriculum studies.

Particular help may be desired in planning programs for classes in special education. Mental retardation, disabilities affecting various sensory modalities, or unusual academic aptitudes pose issues about which psychologists may be expected to make a contribution.

Assistance to school personnel in selecting, revising, and improving group testing programs is a common activity. Knowledge about the availability of group tests, appraisal of the relevance of particular tests to curriculum goals, judgments about the qualities of tests from a technical standpoint, consideration of the uses of results, and aid in training personnel to administer, score, and interpret such tests may be desired. Even if the psychologist is not fully informed in all aspects of group tests, his background in psychology qualifies him as the most appropriate member of the school staff to equip himself to be of service in this connection.

Other specialized personnel. In the pursuit of his duties, the psychologist develops relationships with other specialists on the school staff. Specialists in guidance, remedial reading, speech, social work, or health services may work with the psychologist on a given problem. Because the needs of the case determine which special services are to be involved, flexibility in the relationships among specialists is necessary.

Each discipline defines its responsibility in the school setting as contributing to the learning effectiveness and mental health of the pupil. This common goal gives strength to the educational effort but sometimes leads to conflict about who does what, when. Overlapping in training makes possible many common understandings but also contributes to some overlapping—and therefore potential conflict—in job functions. Since these circumstances are more or less unavoidable, the important issue is how the specialists work together in a particular situation.

If a smoothly functioning team is to result, the job functions and roles of the various specialists must be clarified to their mutual satisfaction. Professional energy must be used to help pupils. The goal of working together effectively is the responsibility of the representatives of each discipline.

Among the specialists, the school psychologist is usually most highly skilled in conducting intensive diagnostic studies. Thus he is likely to be consulted, for example, by the guidance worker or the remedial reading specialist when serious problems of adjustment or difficult issues of assessment arise in the normal course of their work. The specific problem to be studied by the psychologist may be discussed and the results reviewed with the guidance worker or reading teacher who resumes the major role in working with the pupil. On the other hand, the major remedial responsibility may be assumed by the psychologist. Such flexibility in procedures is the hallmark of a harmoniously functioning team of specialists where the welfare of the pupil determines the remedial goals and the procedures for attaining them.

Psychologists typically work closely with such health services personnel as the school physician and nurse. Many behavior difficulties arise in which physical factors are primary or contributing. In any event, such possibilities are examined before more intensive psychological studies are undertaken. The specific channels of referral and consultation are best worked out by the personnel in a given situation.

When the school employs social workers, close cooperation between them and the psychologist is necessary. The training and experience of the social worker in community organization and in family dynamics makes it natural for her to carry responsibility for these areas on the mental health team. Again, the specific responsibilities assumed are best predicated on functional competence rather than on status or job title.

In an increasing number of school systems, psychiatrists are retained on a consultant basis to make available to the psychologist and other staff members their special knowledge and skills. How the psychiatrist works with the group is usually determined by those involved. Frequently, difficult problems of diagnosis are referred to him for assistance. Problems involving complex issues of differential diagnosis are fully appraised by the group to arrive at the best possible judgment. In addition to participating in casework, the psychiatrist may become involved in more general problems of mental health in the schools. Psychiatrists with experience in the schools have frequently remarked how much they had to learn about education, teaching, and the schools in general before they could make a contribution in these areas.

It is encouraging to note the growing interest of many psychiatrists in the potential resources of the schools for promoting the mental health of all pupils. Although the literature on the subject has increased greatly and more and more schools are employing psychiatrists on a consultant basis, no general pattern for the best deployment of psychiatric knowledge and skills has yet emerged. Mental health experts agree that at the present time the schools hold greater promise than any other social institution for developing positive mental health and for the preventing emotional disturbances.

Working with Parents

It is widely recognized that a partnership between parents and the school is necessary for the maximum educational development of the pupil. This ideal is rarely achieved in any given community, yet school personnel would be remiss in their obligations if they did not work to achieve it. In every community there are parents who are indifferent, fearful, or hostile about the schools. There are families whose members are in conflict with other community institutions. These families contribute more than their share of children who pose learning problems for school personnel. Even families with better resources, however, may produce children who have learning or adjustment difficulties. In each of these cases, the necessity of working with parents arises.

When the school perceives a child as having difficulties, parents are likely to be apprehensive and defensive about the special attention being given to the child. The reasons are numerous and are to be found in deeply rooted cultural beliefs as well as in the personal histories of particular parents. Whatever the case may be, the psychologist must be alert to the need of parents for acceptance and understanding under circumstances that are always emotionally charged to some extent. Anger toward the parent out of sympathy for the child does not help establish the working relationship necessary to help the child. Here a professional, objective stance is required, even under provocation. Parents are in a position to provide data about the child's behavior in the home and community that is available from no other source. In conferences, parents reveal themselves—their values, aspirations, and struggles. Such data are useful in understanding the pupil's significant adult and home environment. Thus parents participate in diagnosis to some extent— the kind of collaboration that should be encouraged.

Not only do parents provide data for understanding pupils, but their cooperation is usually necessary to carry out an effective rehabilitation plan. At the same time that the psychologist elicits data about the pupil, he is appraising the context within which a remedial program is to be evolved. There is little point in suggesting to parents actions which they are not able or willing to carry out.

When a social worker is not available, the psychologist may actually visit homes when the parent is unable or unwilling to come to the school.

In many instances, the skillful psychologist wins new friends for the school by overcoming initial parental resistance and contributing to the pupil's development—an aspiration shared by almost all parents, however personally troubled.

Although most conferences with parents begin with the goal of obtaining a comprehensive appraisal of the problems of pupils, they sometimes bring to light the parent's own need for help with personal problems. The psychologist will normally keep the interview focused on the issues directly concerning the pupil, but this is not always easy or possible. In such event, he will recognize that the parent does have a problem for which assistance may be needed and draw upon his knowledge of community resources to refer the parent to an appropriate person or agency. He waits for the parent to express a desire for help, rather than inferring the need from the clinical data available.

Sometimes direct services are provided to parents through short-term individual or group counseling. Helping a parent may, in a given case, be the best way to help a child. No other resource may be available except the school. Questions arise, of course, as to the extent to which the resources of the school should be employed in this way, but decisions on this point must be made according to the factors in particular situations rather than through general prescriptions. The fact is simply reported that in numerous instances parents are given assistance with their problems on the basis that such action will best contribute to the welfare of the children.

The alert psychologist will find many opportunities to assist parents in relation to the education of their children. Psychologists are often requested to address PTA meetings on topics of interest to parents. Parents are usually open to the suggestions of the psychologist, and these pave the way for programs which will clarify and interpret for parents his roles and functions. This may be done in various ways—through lectures, dialogues, or sociodramatic presentation. An opportunity to inform parents about the psychologist's methods should not be neglected. The mystery and apprehension sometimes ascribed to psychological services can be replaced by understanding, with the result that such services may be used more intelligently and will more likely be supported at budget hearings. Furthermore, by establishing friendly relations with parents in this kind of atmosphere, the word gets around that the psychologist is readily approachable rather than one to be seen only in dire emergencies.

In some PTA organizations, child study groups are organized, consisting of parents or of parents and teachers. The psychologist as a specialist in child development may be called upon as a resource person to help guide the study program. Study groups are certainly to be encouraged and assisted by psychologists. In some situations, psychologists have been known to exercise initiative and leadership in organizing such groups.

Psychologists may also be called upon to assist teachers with parent-teacher conferences. They may be consulted about preparation for the conference in terms of interpretation of the data available in the personnel records. In special instances, when difficult problems are expected to arise, they may be invited to sit in on the conference. Teachers generally take the lead in making such arrangements and the psychologist as a consultant is available as needed. After a conference is concluded, the teacher may wish to confer with the psychologist to discuss some particularly difficult or baffling problem which arose while it was going on.

A common problem in parent-teacher conferences is how to keep the discussion focused on the objective of the interview and avoid digressions into the parents' personal problems. One teacher brought such a problem to the psychologist for consultation. He asked her for a detailed description of the entire conference. Since he was not involved in the conference, the psychologist could be rather objective about evaluating it. He noted first, that the teacher had failed to make clear to the parent the purposes of the conference. As a result she had no baseline to which to return when the discussion seemed to veer from the topic. Without a stated goal, she could not point out to the parent that her problems, however important or interesting, were not particularly germane to the objectives of the conference.

A second point that became evident was the teacher's fear of displeasing the parent by giving unfavorable information about the child's progress. This led to a discussion as to whether such conferences were intended to mollify the parent or to face frankly the data at hand and work out the best possible plan for assisting the child. Since we can assume that the psychologist fulfilled his role skillfully, we may conclude that the consultation proved helpful to the teacher in helping her understand what had happened as well as in providing her with clues for the improvement of subsequent sessions.

Working with Community Mental Health Resources

Not all the resources required to promote the mental health of pupils are to be found within the province of the school system. Indeed it is rare to find such sufficiency within the school. The remarkable development of mental health as a social movement since the turn of the century has led to the establishment of a broad spectrum of services potentially available for use by the schools. Community guidance clinics, family agencies, facilities in general hospitals, residential treatment centers, and private practitioners representing the mental health professions of psychiatry, psychology, and social work constitute rather specialized resources of considerable relevance to the schools. In addition, other community agencies and institutions—whose primary purpose is not mental health service per se—may in a given instance have orientations, interests, and facilities of particular value to the school psychologist. These may include the church, the courts, and the police, health, and welfare departments of the local government.

If the variety of resources is to be skillfully exploited in the service of the schools, someone on the school staff must assume responsibility for assembling and keeping up-to-date functional information about agencies which serve children, youths, and families. Sometimes help is not given simply because no one knows about the available resources. This role may, in some instances, be delegated to a social worker, or it may be shared by various staff members on a coordinated basis.

It is not enough merely to compile a directory of community agencies. In many communities a social welfare council or mental health association may already have prepared such a listing. The school mental health consultant or liaison person must establish personal contact with a staff member of the agency and learn in some detail about the particular kind of assistance available, as well as about costs, waiting lists, and anything else that will facilitate effective working relationships between school and agency for the welfare of pupils and families. Learning about resources is a continuous task, for changes in purposes and personnel may occur over a period of time.

In many communities the complaint is heard that facilities lack over-all coordination and that jurisdictional rivalries and competition among agencies exist. Although this may be true, the psychologist nevertheless seeks to maintain the best possible relationship on a professional basis, in order to assist pupils. The school staff must be helped to appreciate the fact that referral processes may require considerable skill in interpersonal and interprofessional relationships, and that these relationships take time to develop. It is also an accepted principal that responsibility for developing and maintaining such relationships is best located in one person, rather than divided among many staff members.

There may be private practitioners, qualified in the fields of psychology, psychiatry, or social work, who offer therapeutic services for children and youth. Local professional associations can often be helpful in identifying such persons. Card files containing such information as training and experience, types of therapeutic services, age-groups preferred, and fee schedules will prove useful in matching resource to client need as effectively as possible.

Use of outside resources must be evaluated on a continuing basis to determine the extent to which services have been effective. Although it is usually difficult to obtain valid and reliable evidence, the effort is definitely worthwhile. In the long run, evaluation procedures provide the best basis for continued use of resources by the schools. By maintaining a close relationship with the personnel of an outside agency, the school psychologist may provide information which will enable the agency to improve its contribution to pupils receiving its services. If we remember that people often resist critical evaluation of their performance, the sensitivity of this function of the psychologist may be appreciated.

Thus far we have stressed some of the functions of the psychologist as he reaches outward from the schools to find assistance for pupils. The other facet of the liaison function refers to roles within the school community. The psychologist seeks to interpret for his colleagues, generally or in the context of a particular case, the nature, possibilities, and limitations of outside help. If a pupil is receiving assistance outside the school, it may be very important for the teacher or other persons working with the pupil within the school to be informed about or have interpreted for them the nature of the assistance and its implications for ongoing tasks in the classroom. If a pupil is receiving therapeutic assistance, for example, it can be useful for the teacher to understand that the previously shy youngster may become somewhat aggressive before a better level of stability is achieved. Recommendation for temporary adjustments in expectations of performance certainly will be more effectively carried out when the teacher sees the meaning of the recommendation. She will more readily perceive the importance of her share in the total helping process.

There are instances when the teacher may be involved directly with the helping agency. She may be invited to participate in the case conference at the community guidance center when an assessment is being made and a total treatment program developed. She may have periodic conferences with an agency representative, such as the social worker. The patterns of effective relation between school and community agency are likely to vary among school systems and indeed even from case to case. There is no basis for a contention that one way of working is necessarily superior to others; the essential criterion is the welfare of the pupil.

The enterprising psychologist does not limit his mental health liaison role to knowledge about and effective use of existing community resources. He also exerts leadership in better use and coordination of existing facilities to help them better serve the schools. Personnel of agencies may report that they do not understand enough about the purposes and programs of the school to maximize their contributions to the school community. They are likely to be properly reticent about taking the initiative toward such improvements. As a representative of the school, the psychologist may take the initiative in expressing the desire of the schools for cooperative relationships. If his approach is sound, he is likely to find a receptive audience.

If time, energy, and imagination are available, the leadership role may go farther. The psychologist may join the local mental health association to work with citizens in the development of needed community facilities. Participation in programs of community mental health education, and work on committees to stimulate citizens as well as private and public agencies toward a larger commitment for mental health services will, in the long view, be a real service to the schools. In such a role, too, the psychologist is in a position to help educate the public to a more constructive perspective of the strategic potentialities of the schools for the mental health of all children. What is said in this connection, of course, is also applicable to administrators, teachers, and other members of the school staff.

Recent years have seen interesting developments in which local government agencies such as the police, health, and welfare departments, and the courts may work more closely with the schools to ameliorate and, hopefully, to prevent behavior difficulties of pupils. There is room for much experimentation along these lines, focused on the central objective of enabling the schools to carry out their mission.

The juvenile conference committee is an example of a youth-serving agency which works cooperatively with schools. Under the general supervision of the juvenile court judge, a local community may organize a committee of citizens whose quasilegal function is defined in the area of pre-delinquent detection and correction. Representative citizens with an interest in and talent for working with youth are recruited to deal with minor offenses which may initiate careers of delinquency if not corrected early. Offenses not serious enough to warrant immediate court adjudication may be referred by the police for study and remedial action. Businessmen, professional persons, housewives, and others who comprise the committee work with the offender, his parents, and other community agencies to obtain a clear picture of the reasons for the unacceptable behavior and to develop a plan to assure that the behavior will not be likely to recur. In the course of the deliberations the school psychologist may become involved as the school liaison person both to offer technical counsel as a psychologist and to coordinate community efforts with the school program.

An example is the case of two boys who were apprehended by the police for vandalism. Since it was a first offense and since the families were interested and eager to help, the case was referred to the committee for evaluation and possible action. In conducting its study, the committee consulted the psychologist about the school conduct of the boys. The report was entirely favorable up to the time of the offense. The boys and the parents were interviewed and it appeared that there was some laxity on the part of the parents in supervising the leisure activities of the boys. Since the offenders were eager to make amends, and all of the factors appeared favorable to changes in parental management, the case was referred to parental custody and correction. In this instance the parents asked for permission to confer with the school psychologist for further counsel in guidance of the boys if necessary.

Other cases with comparable constructive outcomes could be cited to justify the excellent work being done by this kind of school-community cooperation.

Another area of great promise in furthering the mental health of children and youth is found in the growing collaboration between schools and clergymen in the community. Field studies have shown that for many problems people are more likely to seek the counsel of their clergyman than of other professionals. Thus the clergy are frequently in a position to learn about family crises affecting children earlier than other persons or institutions. If working relationships have been established between the clergy and mental health personnel in the school—often the psychologist—there is greater likelihood that, when appropriate, incipient problems of children may be brought to the attention of the school.

Cooperation is a two-way street. Many psychologists have found it very valuable to involve clergymen in assessment and remedial programs. The assistance of the clergy has been found in some instances to be crucial in reaching parents and eliciting their participation for helping their children. The same point might be made about carrying out remedial programs involving other members of the family. As both the clergy and school psychologists become more sensitive to the values that might accrue from closer working relationships, newer patterns of mutual assistance may be expected to evolve. The potentialities have hardly been tapped.

The reservoirs of assistance inherent in many facets of community life for the promotion of mental health in pupils are far greater than have been realized. Although it can be argued that the initiative for exploiting such resources should lie outside the schools, in any given situation the leadership will emerge where there is sensitivity and a desire to leave no stone unturned to mobilize help for the needy pupil. It is a tribute indeed to the school that on many an unheralded occasion, compassion, intelligence, and action were found there, and many a child has been helped while sideline philosophers debated as to where the duty lay.

CHAPTER VI

Educator Roles

The educational role of the school psychologist is usually ranked low in studies of his current role functions. Often he is so busy meeting the requirements of other roles, such as in psychodiagnosis and remedial activities, or in consultation, that there is little time for educational activities. Psychologists themselves may not fully realize the potential gains from greater attention to this role. The term *educator role* is used here to refer to the role of the psychologist in providing more formal opportunities for the teacher to improve her knowledge of the theories and practices of psychology which will enable her better to discharge her functions as a teacher.

For several reasons this situation is unfortunate. It is at least an article of faith that psychology can contribute much toward raising the general level of teacher knowledge about human growth and development, which would in turn be reflected in greater excellence in teaching and learning. Furthermore, the teacher is in the front lines in detecting early signs of intellectual, social, and emotional defects and can profit by a deeper knowledge of psychological theory and practice concerning behavioral deviations.

It is the purpose of this chapter to make a case for a greater allotment of the time of the psychologist to bring the benefits of psychology and other behavioral sciences to bear upon the multifaceted educational enterprise. It is accepted that administrators and supervisors also have a significant responsibility in providing leadership in teacher development.

Education of Teachers

Although it is proper to focus on making the learning environment of pupils as stimulating and challenging as possible, we sometimes forget that one of the best learning situations for pupils is one in which teachers are excited about their own learning. Excitement about new insights and growth is contagious. Teachers who are learners, who are searching for more knowledge about themselves, about students, and about their areas of scholarly interest, will present an image of learning that cannot fail to have positive effects on pupils. When teachers follow routine procedures year after year and act as if all truth about teaching had already been discovered, they are likely to have a deadening effect on the inquiring spirit of their students.

The point has previously been made that the psychologist, whether working with the teacher on the problems of a particular pupil or in consultation on a variety of more general issues, is alert to help teachers derive principles of general application in their work. His philosophy of a helping relationship is to work with teachers in particular instances so that their knowledge and skill are strengthened for future challenges. Growth may take many forms—greater appreciation of the variety of normal behavior in nine-year-olds, more knowledge of specific ways of studying individual pupils, keener awareness of possibilities for individualizing instruction in the regular classroom, deeper insight into how a teacher's own attitudes affect the behavior of some pupils, and so on. Although this kind of "tutorial" assistance can yield deeply personal and significant learnings within the context of a relationship, there are also other kinds of learning to be pursued on a more systematic basis.

To be effective, programs should be based upon careful identification of teacher needs. As a result of numerous contacts with teachers while conducting assessment studies, carrying through remedial procedures, or consulting on a variety of classroom problems, the psychologist may become aware of gaps in teacher knowledge about motivation, learning, personality, group behavior, and the like, which may serve as areas for more formal study.

From an analysis of the kinds of referral made, the psychologist may become alert to the recurrent needs of teachers to improve their methods of observing and describing pupil behavior more objectively and reliably. Or data on the referral forms may suggest a need for better ways for theorizing about behavior from available evidence. The psychologist looks not for the needs of individual teachers, but for issues of general and recurrent nature upon which a program of study for a group might be constructed. The data might suggest need to focus on the referral form itself to improve it as a medium of communication.

A systematic survey of teachers' perceived needs might serve as a takeoff for programming. The survey might be of the free response type, or structured in advance by listing topics, questions, or problems to permit the staff to indicate preferences. Suggestions for type of training procedures, duration of program, available meeting time, and other information might be elicited. Although these methods are likely to have limitations, one of them may be suitable for starting a program.

If a course or seminar is established, it should not be in the nature of a university course transplanted to a school system. For example, a course in child development should be more than the usual course with a textbook and other course routines. It should be based upon the real questions that have been stimulated by the efforts of teachers to work with youngsters. During undergraduate study, topics such as individual differences, learning, motivation, or discipline were considered as abstractions. To the active teacher, however, these issues are invested with personal meaning, with feelings of success or failure, with anxieties about self-esteem. The problems are real, the abstractions have come alive, the words have acquired existential significance. If the teachers take their questions seriously, the leader will have few problems of motivating members of the seminar. To be faced by a group of zealous learners may, however, prove threatening to the psychologist. His own abstractions will not satisfy eager appetites. He, too, will have to draw upon experience beyond the printed word. He may wish he were back in the safety of the clinic!

To deal with the living issues brought in by teachers, all of the knowledge that can be mustered from the various fields of psychology may be needed and tested for relevance to current problems. The old packaging of knowledge with labels such as "learning," "developmental," "social," "clinical," "psychometrics," and "personality" may prove to be inappropriate.

One might conceive of a course in developmental psychology which would include teachers from all grades. All the teachers might profit from a deeper perspective growing out of a longitudinal study of development to counteract the artifacts of believing that developmental imperatives are guided by grade levels. Some of the preconceptions that teachers of different grade levels sometimes hold toward one another might be challenged. In one situation where this approach was tried, each participant carried out a case study of a pupil or a group and, during the course of the seminar, reported her findings to the group for discussion. It was interesting to observe how the comments of teachers tended to be colored by their specialized information about the particular age group with which they normally worked. Awareness of this limitation led a fifth-grade teacher to want to know more about junior high youngsters. It also led a high school teacher to wonder what her tenth-graders were like in their early years. Although the seminar was held in a small school system, some of the teachers remarked on how little contact they had had with one another over the years.

Another result of the post-seminar evaluation was the frequent statement that difficulties in teaching are *not* related to grade level. The tendency to ascribe problems in higher grades to defects in teaching in lower grades was not evident in the seminar group. This fact made everyone wonder whether present designs of grade organization have built barriers between teachers and obstructed communication. The approach of forming study groups was viewed as a step in the direction of improved communication and understanding.

One of the most popular and effective educational devices used with teachers is the case conference method. Each participating teacher is expected to select one pupil from her class for intensive study over a period of time. She is likely to choose a pupil who represents some problem in teaching. She may use classroom observation, tests, cumulative records, interviews, learning products (such as art work), and the like. The data are studied to generate hypotheses about certain aspects of the pupil's behavior. The usual processes of testing hypotheses, revising them, and collecting more data are used.

The focus on a particular pupil normally increases the motivation and ego-involvement of the teacher in the learning process. As the participants consider case presentations, their personal reactions often come to the fore and become a focus for discussion. It is discovered that the understanding of a pupil may involve consideration of the teacher's feelings and actions toward him. Thus the pupil-teacher relationship, as well as the individual pupil, may be seen as a unit of study.

Discovery, recognition, and acceptance of one's mode of relating to a pupil may be seen as having wider application. Another outcome may be improvement in methods of studying pupils. Systematic, objective, and reliable observation of pupils may be seen as likely to improve the quality of instructional decisions in meeting the individual differences of pupils. Furthermore, questions about the utility of psychological theories for understanding behavior are bound to arise, for it is apparent that methods of study are no substitute for teacher acumen in asking questions, nor do they provide automatic conclusions upon which the teacher can eventually act.

The case method may also be applied to the study of groups. A teacher may select her entire class for study. Characteristics about the group members may be assembled to describe the distributions of ability, achievement, and aptitudes. Surveys of interests and attitudes may be made. Data about socio-economic background, recreational preferences, or out-of-school activities may be compiled. Various sociometric devices may be administered for insight into the social structure of the class. The purpose is not, of course, merely to collect data, but to develop a background which can be useful in making educational decisions. Teachers who have given time to such systematic studies have reported that the time invested pays off later in teaching efficiency and in better guidance of pupils and the group.

The case conference contains no magic; leadership is vital in helping the participants to work as a group as well as in providing assistance on individual projects. The group's success will not depend solely upon the person whose initiative brought it into being, but upon the extent to which all participants accept responsibility for making the group what they want it to be.

A program of study obviously need not wait until all teachers are interested. It may be better to begin with a group which is well-motivated; others who hesitate at first may become curious, especially if they hear enthusiastic reports about the program, and become interested later on.

Continuous evaluation of any program is essential to improving it and keeping it vital. If the purpose for which a particular course or seminar is organized is achieved, the group should be prepared to dissolve unless another goal derives from the earlier one. In a functional program there is nothing sacred about the length of time devoted to a subject or problem. If the processes involved in the seminar capture the imagination, one can imagine that one problem will lead to another and maintain an excitement in learning. Perhaps the knowledge that adjournment is in its hands stimulates a group to continued growth!

The psychologist may not limit his program to the self-perceived needs of teachers at a given time. He may wish to bring to their attention new developments in psychology and other behavioral sciences which have significance for teaching. Recent advances in the psychology of learning, psychometrics, programmed learning and teaching machines, or group dynamics may be offered as possible topics for in-service programs. The teacher can hardly aspire to keep abreast of developments in theory, research, and practice in the many fields that may be of value to her. Although he should be alert to new developments, the psychologist should not be expected to be competent to offer instruction in all the specialties involved. He may be able to draw upon nearby universities or other community institutions for expert assistance.

The school may draw pupils from a heterogeneous community in which conflicting social forces are at work. Recent research has raised questions about class-related definitions of mental health and adjustment now in use. The "unmotivated" pupil may reflect social values in his behavior which cannot be understood merely in personality terms. A seminar might be organized to be led by a sociologist or social anthropologist to gain insight into some of these issues. Study of community influences on families may disclose differential value structures which create problems in school. An analysis of cultural cross currents in the community may reveal unsuspected relationships between family pressures and pupil behavior. A more clearly differentiated picture of the ways in which community factors are reflected in the school may add a new dimension to teaching, and make it more vital and realistic.

In one school system a program was planned to call attention to the potential implications of developments in the computer field for education. In cooperation with a business firm operating in this field, lectures, demonstrations, visual aids, and discussions were employed to present current achievements and future prospects to the entire school staff. Implications for teaching, record keeping, communication systems, and curriculum content were considered with great interest and enthusiasm.

In addition to face-to-face programs as described in this chapter, other techniques are available. A department of psychology in one school issues regular reports to all personnel. Summaries of recent research or annotated bibliographies are compiled for use by special groups within the school staff. Interpretations and illustrations of its own work and discussions of techniques of interest to teachers are included from time to time.

The enterprising school psychologist will find many avenues for discharging a meaningful educator role once the conviction about its importance and value develops.

Staff Training and Development

The application of principles and procedures of group dynamics to the professional growth of educational personnel has had an exciting development during the past two decades. Even when initial enthusiasm for the "miracles" of group dynamics has subsided, there remains a solid residue of principles and practice that bear great relevance to education, for so many staff activities are carried out in groups.

Consider some of the following: faculty meetings, case conferences, faculty study groups concerned with a variety of school- or systemwide problems, parent-teacher meetings, and departmental conferences suggest the variety of group activities carried on within the educational system. On occasions such meetings are productive and satisfying to participants; at other times they are unproductive and boring, leaving their participants with a sense of frustration or pessimism about the possibilities of group effectiveness.

In the search for principles underlying the functions of groups, much has been learned. Criteria for healthily functioning groups have been developed. Techniques for appraising the effectiveness of groups, and remedial procedures for improving them, have been devised. At least a start has been made in helping people learn how to make groups function more effectively.

The school psychologist who has acquired skills in this area will find many opportunities to exercise them. In most instances his role will be that of consultant. Except in the event that he himself heads a staff of specialists, he has no direct responsibility for staff leadership and administration. In most situations, he will have to let it become known that he has an interest and special competence to offer to those who may be interested in improving their group procedures. He cannot force himself upon a group.

However, even in those circumstances in which he is an occasional participant in ad hoc groups or has been appointed to a continuing group, he may find opportunities to generate the interest of other members in staff improvement. By his own participation in a group, the psychologist may exemplify good "member" behavior or good "leadership" behavior, as the occasion warrants. Or he may suggest procedures which will improve the group's behavior when it bogs down. In many subtle ways he may encourage group members to develop an interest in studying their own behavior. When widespread interest develops, he may assume greater leadership in suggesting methods of group self-study and improvement.

If the psychologist is called in as a "trouble-shooter" by the group leader, he will seek to determine the readiness of others in the group to carry on a program of study and improvement. He will be aware of some of the materials of self-study now available and bring them to the attention of the group. Above all his approach must be flexible; he must be prepared to begin where the group is at the time and reflect a hopeful attitude that effort by the group may lead to fruitful results.

A practice of long standing within education is the holding of regular faculty meetings. Criticisms and complaints about the dreariness and lack of accomplishment of faculty meetings are commonplace among both teachers and administrators. As with the weather, the view is held that nothing can be done except to endure them. Recent developments in applied social psychology suggest that a great deal can be done to improve the procedures and products of any group which can be motivated toward such ends. No doubt the first step is to face discontent and replace it with a desire for improvement. This is the task of leadership, wherever it may be found—in an administrator, a teacher, or a psychologist. There are reports in the literature which support the view that substantial gains in group productivity and satisfaction are possible when groups address themselves to these objectives.

It is unfortunately true that groups are often formed before there has been a clear determination of the problem to be solved or without consideration as to whether a solution may best be achieved by a group. Disenchantment may result in either event. Some kinds of problems can be more expeditiously handled by other means.

One of the most frequent complaints of faculty members is the amount of time required for committee meetings about a myriad of issues. If we can concede that a certain amount of committee work is essential for the effective transaction of school affairs, we can then ask: How can the quality of committee work be improved? The problem may be conceived as one of helping individuals learn how to function in groups in order to improve the quality of group work. At least two approaches are feasible.

If the psychologist is skilled in group procedures, he may join certain committees with the express purpose of helping them to improve their ways of working. He will serve as a consultant, concentrating on problem-solving procedures rather than on the substantive issues before the group. He may encounter initial resistance since he is perceived as an "outsider" without direct responsibility to contribute to the end product of committee work. Let us assume that this problem does not arise, or that it has been satisfactorily resolved. At the outset, he may challenge the group to formulate as clearly as it can the task before it. Some committees run into difficulty because they do not spend time in developing a clear definition of their mission. A committee established "to improve science instruction in the middle grades" will probably have a pretty vague idea of its task. Time must be given to stating in clear and concrete terms the nature of the group's mission, or later problems will surely arise.

When the goal is clearly in view, the consultant may direct his attention to the means by which the committee seeks to reach its goals. Does it have the necessary information? What more is needed? Who shall obtain it? Do the members of the group have the necessary competencies for problem-solving? As the group carries on its deliberations, the psychologist may observe the patterns of participation, or make notes about the leadership style and techniques of the chairman. He will share his observations as facts, without interpretation, when it appears that a look at its own procedures may be profitable for the group. As the members feel more secure with one another and come to accept him as one of the group, he may be asked for interpretations about particular aspects of the group's functioning. He may then point out how some of the observed behaviors facilitate problem-solving and how other behaviors impede it. He may use illustrations to point to ways for improving the procedures of certain individuals or of the entire group.

At times, the committee might be asked to stop its normal activity for a training session focused on a special problem. To illustrate how particular leader behavior produces effects on group members, a sociodramatic technique may be employed. Or one of the training films now available might be viewed and discussed, with applications to the group itself. If such activity seems to divert the group from its appointed task, it should be remembered that the lessons that may be learned in this context are expected to generalize to later sessions and to future committee work, and in the long run to lead to greater productivity and satisfaction.

As the sessions proceed, the consultant may suggest that time be taken to evaluate progress toward goals, as well as to look at what members are learning about their own behavior. The self-consciousness thus generated may be expected to diminish with experience.

An alternative to the approach described is to set up training sessions, under the guidance of the consultant, in which group procedures are studied in more concentrated fashion. Simulated problems with high reality value may be used to good effect. Many of the procedures discussed above will also be employed here. Sessions may run as long as they are fruitful, and new groups may be formed at any time. One of the encouraging aspects of training in this field is that almost everyone participating will make some progress in improving the quality of his behavior in groups.

In larger school systems, where there are many psychologists or where special services personnel are organized into a department or service administered by a psychologist, the psychologist has a particular responsibility for the continuing professional development of the personnel. Regular staff meetings are the common medium employed. It is important here, too, for the group to formulate explicitly its aims and expectations and devise the best means for achieving them. Problems in administration and coordination among various staff members, consideration of problem cases, and discussions of substantive issues in the respective specialties represented are likely focuses at different times. High morale in the group is a probable outcome of efforts to understand and help one another solve problems of all kinds. It is always tragic to discover that a group of persons supposedly somewhat expert in interpersonal relationships may not apply to its own functions the knowledge of the group's stock in trade.

Since special service personnel are no less human than others, one would expect problems of status, jurisdictional conflicts, and difficulties in personal relationships to occur. However, it is a reasonable expectation that this group will actively confront the issues and seek solutions.

In some situations the psychologist may find it advisable to seek the services of outside consultants to assist in some aspects of staff development. He may not be sufficiently knowledgeable and skillful in this area, and no one else on the school staff may have the needed competence. An outsider may bring a fresh perspective and may not be encumbered by previously developed attitudes and assumptions. Industry, particularly, has successfully pioneered in this respect and its reported experience may well be worth critical review by educators and school psychologists.

Psychology has made greater progress in the theory and practice of understanding and improving individual behavior than it has with respect to group behavior. Yet, in the past two decades particularly, the advances in theories about group and organizational behavior (interactions among groups and collective behavior) have been most promising. In addition, practical measures for studying and modifying group behavior have been devised.

CHAPTER VII

Research Roles

In the past, research has played a relatively minor role in the regular activity of the school psychologist. The same situation prevails today, but the prospects for an enlarged role in the future are encouraging.

Research on Educational Problems

The view has long been held that the discovery of new knowledge is mainly the responsibility of the university. Atlhough there is considerable validity to this position, recent decades have seen governmental agencies and business enterprises become involved in research and make substantial contributions. To be sure, a common pattern has developed in which collaborative effort between universities and other institutions has been productive. In many places collaboration has also occurred between universities and school systems. Probably no one would argue, however, that the research potential within education has been realized. In fact, from the perspective of the vast research laboratory which our far-flung, richly varied school systems could become, we have done relatively little to exploit our opportunities.

It would not be possible, or perhaps even profitable, to identify the reasons for this state of affairs. Public attitudes toward schools as service institutions, lack of leadership and financial support, perhaps even lack of ideas, have probably been deterrents. But the situation is gradually changing. New respect for scientific method and attitudes as instrumental to our survival as a society is emerging. Perhaps even a product of the educational system itself, the nurturance and strengthening of methods of experimental inquiry slowly gain ground. To some this perspective may seem overoptimistic, even romantic, but it can be defended. At the very least, faith in scientific method to solve problems is strongly preferred to reliance upon authority and tradition.

93

It would be difficult indeed to obtain agreement about distinctions between basic and applied research in education. Whatever the distinctions are, both are essential. In some areas a useful distinction may be made. For example, studies in learning processes in a variety of animals and in humans has led to a particular theory of learning by Skinner and his associates at Harvard University. Since the initial goal of the study was to determine the lawful dimensions of learning phenomena, it may be regarded as basic research. The attempt today to use these principles of learning in teaching machines and programmed textbooks may be regarded as applications. Then the issue arises about the effectiveness of these methods for various kinds of subjects in contrast to alternative methods. Inquiry into comparative effects might be called applied research.

As another illustration, study of the processes by which children learn to read may lead to formulation of a particular theory or set of tentative principles. The problem then remains to apply such principles in practical situations and study the consequences under controlled conditions.

The point stressed here is that we need theories, applications, and studies of the effects of application in almost every aspect of the educational enterprise if we are to improve it. As with all large-scale enterprises, it cannot be studied whole; we must select particular problems, develop hypotheses, gather data under appropriate conditions, study effects, and revise our theories and practices. And so it goes, on and on. No final solutions are expected, only incremental improvements.

It would be presumptuous to argue that research is the prerogative of the school psychologist. Because of his training, however, he may reasonably be expected to have a hand in it in relation to his competence to provide leadership. It should be frankly admitted that some school psychologists do not have special training in research, although the situation is gradually changing. At present, because of the service demands of the school and the shortage of psychologists, relatively little research has been conducted by school psychologists.

In a sense, this chapter considers what might be—in fact, what is likely to be—as more psychologists are trained at more advanced levels. This precaution is necessary lest expectations be generated which cannot be fulfilled. In larger school systems, particularly in big cities, research psychologists are employed to devote major attention to the study of educational problems and to offer consultation services to others conducting research on a part-time basis.

One of the characteristics of fundamental research, basic or applied, is that the results may be generalized to situations beyond those immediately under scrutiny. Research outcomes which satisfy this requirement are obviously of very great importance. The kinds of studies that might be made are limited only by the imagination of researchers, apart from practical considerations. Studies of learning processes, grouping procedures, teaching effects, remedial work, communication processes, and administrative organization would surely be almost universally useful.

The type of research must of course be appropriate to the situation. The fact that schools are ongoing social systems means that research of the kind performed in the relative isolation of university laboratories is not likely to be feasible. Controls of the type possible in laboratories are not practicable in a school system. Perhaps it is best that research in the schools and in the university laboratory be complementary, each contributing to the larger understanding which integrates all kinds of research.

Action Research

As used here, action research refers to studies which may improve decision-making in the schools. Whatever one's role—administrator, supervisor, teacher, or special staff member—situations occur regularly wherein choices among alternatives must be made within a dynamic social system. Improvement in the quality of choice of decision is an ever-present challenge.

The administration may be considering the introduction of a new policy regarding homogeneous grouping, or the placement of mentally retarded pupils, or a revision of the grading system, or the introduction of French in the third grade. The psychologist, among others, may be invited to participate in the process. A number of questions may arise. Does the literature contain studies and experience reports which may be relevant to the present situation and from which we can learn? What information should be obtained within the present school system that will provide the best basis for a decision? What would be the attitudes of teachers, parents, or whoever else might be affected by a decision? How may we anticipate the possible effects of alternative courses of action? What kinds of data should be collected, by what means, and over what period of time, in order to evaluate the effects of the decision finally made?

These questions illustrate some of the issues that will arise in the minds of those sensitive and committed to the possibilities inherent in scientific attitude and method as a way to improve operational procedures.

Consider the supervisor who is genuinely puzzled about the likely effects of different approaches to helping teachers in individual situations. Since this supervisor works with many teachers, she might decide to work differently with two groups on a planned basis and study the results in a somewhat more systematic manner than is usually the case. Although she cannot readily contrive a neatly designed laboratory-type study with experimental manipulation of one variable, she can take some steps which may provide an evidential basis for preferring one technique of supervision over another. Some one has said that scientific inquiry is refined common sense. No doubt the elements of scientific inquiry were present in the supervisor's earlier attempts to reflect about her experience and arrive at a decision. By working differently in defined ways with predetermined groups of teachers and by regularly recording data about the consequences, she is introducing a measure of refinement which will enable her to reach a sound conclusion.

Suppose a guidance counselor wonders about the effects of certain procedures, or a librarian questions the effects of visible displays upon the circulation of certain classes of books, or the superintendent of a school may be curious about the extent to which communication efforts in the form of circulars or bulletins are read by the public. Cannot any or all of these questions be subjected to empirical study, if the question is important and the cost reasonable?

Perhaps more decisions are made in the classroom than in any other part of the school system. Teaching might be conceived as an almost continuous series of decisions. Poor teaching may be the regular making of the same decisions without regard to consequences. If a teacher were asked to name the aspects of the job which puzzle her, they would most surely be reducible to issues of decision-making in advancing the learning of students.

As an illustration, let us assume that a teacher is interested in improving the efficiency of her methods for evaluating pupil progress. She may restrict her interest at the start to a determination of the relative efficiency of several methods for evaluating the range of information about the subject matter of the course. After preliminary study and consultation, she decides to compare multiple choice, true-false, and essay-type formats in relation to potential coverage of material. It is not our purpose here to design a study, but to indicate that research approaches to classroom problems are entirely feasible. The teacher, however, may need expert consultation to help her with technical aspects of the effort. The goal is to improve her own practices over time; there is no intention of arriving at conclusions with broad application.

The philosophy and practice of action-oriented research may be implemented by individuals or groups. Frequently, several teachers are interested in a similar kind of problem or in a problem that affects them all, and may elect to work cooperatively toward research solutions. The psychologist may well be a member of such a group, offering his special competence in research techniques as well as in group procedures.

Consultation Services

The discussion about research thus far suggests at least two research roles for the school psychologist. He may design and execute research questions of his own choice or those referred to him by others, and he may serve as consultant to others in various phases of their own research activity. In either event, he exemplifies to others a conception of the importance of the research method for attacking problems of educational significance. Talks, however eloquent, about the values of research rarely motivate others to initiate it. Reluctance to do research may spring from many sources: the lack of conviction, or training, or time, the belief that research is for the experts, or the view that many questions cannot be approached through research.

Although these obstacles may be formidable indeed, the psychologist who wishes to do so can make progress if he keeps one important consideration in mind. As long as there are questions in the minds of members of the school staff, the ground is fertile for initiating various research procedures for helping to answer them.

Consultation involves more than announcing one's availability to anyone interested. The psychologist must participate actively in the ongoing dialogue within the school about matters of educational importance. As he works with teachers and administrators in meaningful ways, he is very likely to become aware of their concerns, their problematic situations, and their desire for the best possible answers to troublesome questions. Opportunity is in the eye of the beholder.

It was pointed out in Chapter III that intelligent diagnostic study begins with the formulation of the question in a form that permits observation. The same requirement holds for research. The query, "How may I improve my methods of evaluating pupil progress?" requires further exploration and specification before observations can be made. It is important to remember that this process of exploration and formulation of the issues in answerable form is an integral part of research itself. The teacher involved in this process who may wonder, "But when will we ever get to do the research?" should be reminded, "You are already doing it."

Consultative services are characterized both by availability and outreach. The psychologist on the staff may not have all the competencies necessary to meet the research requirements of a school system. A common practice in such situations is to retain outside consultants with the particular expertness needed. They are most readily found in nearby colleges and universities. The kinds of cooperative relationships to be developed depend upon the particular situation. Regular consultation in the schools, seminars, or workshops in the school or college, subsidy of a staff member with leave to obtain special training, and formal projects with foundation support are methods which have been used in the past.

It was suggested earlier that some of the points made in this chapter may appear to be pious hopes. The fact that everything suggested has been tried successfully somewhere, sometime, lends support to the belief that the activities are in the realm of the possible. Stress on the potential role, even the obligation, of the psychologist arises from the fact that he represents a scientific as well as a professional discipline. Although many psychologists do not have the training or interest to carry forward the view here advocated, the situation is gradually changing.

Research Services

The psychology staff or department may render direct research services to the school system. Through the department's own initiative or at the suggestion of others, specific questions or issues may be considered for which research study or investigation will provide the best answers. Since such services are likely to require personnel, equipment, and facilities, clear provision must be made in the school policy and budget; otherwise the functions can easily be sidetracked by requests for other kinds of service. Somehow, research activity never seems as urgent as direct help to persons and may be too readily brushed aside.

It may be helpful to illustrate some of the types of services which psychologists might contribute to the better functioning of school systems.

Group testing norms.   Use of group testing programs to provide systematic data about the ability, achievement, and aptitude of pupils has become a widespread practice in school systems. In order to understand the results for a given pupil, it is necessary to compare his performance with that of others. To do this, norms are essential. If the published norms are to be used, the characteristics of the groups upon which the norms were established must be compared with the characteristics of the local school population.

Assume that the distributions of achievement in the local schools are higher than those reported in the manual. Assume further that one is interested in the relationship between ability and achievement. The question arises as to whether the local population also has higher ability levels than the standardization group. In order to study the relationship between ability and achievement in the local school population, it becomes desirable to develop local norms.

It is also necessary to appraise the relevance of the curriculum objectives inherent in national achievement norms to the objectives in a particular school system.

To deal with these questions in a systematic and technically competent manner, the services of the psychologist are called upon. Since the issues involved will require continuing scrutiny over a period of time, it becomes necessary to allocate services on a regular basis.

Reviews of research.   Questions often occur with respect to pending administrative decisions on policy. What does published research have to say about the problem of grouping pupils for advanced classes? What type of program should be adopted? The psychologist is requested to review existing research and make recommendations to school officials. Even if no decisive conclusions are possible from the literature, a review of the research bearing upon the issues can be useful to the superintendent in discussing matters with the local board of education.

Controversy may exist with respect to methods of teaching reading, or the use of reading readiness tests in primary grades. The psychologist may be asked to examine the literature and present the position considered most reasonable on the basis of available theory and research.

Study of dropouts. A school may become concerned about the number of dropouts in the secondary school. Numerous questions may be of interest. What is the dropout rate? What are the characteristics of pupils who leave school early? What was the nature of their performance while in school? Why did they leave? What happens to them? In order to evaluate the answers to some of these questions, it will be necessary to obtain comparable data from groups of pupils who do not drop out.

It soon becomes apparent that a competent investigation of this problem will require personnel, time, and equipment. Although this kind of research may be assigned to a committee of school staff members, the psychologist will be expected to play a leading role in designing and executing the study.

No presumption is made that all questions that may be considered in the light of educational research should be referred to the psychologist. Where the questions are psychological in character, however, and critical interpretation of the research involves an understanding of the conditions and limitations of the research methods used by psychologists, it appears reasonable that the psychologist may be the most competent person to perform the service.

The kinds of research services illustrated here by no means exhaust the possibilities. Whether issues confronting a school system are to be dealt with through research or through the less dependable procedures frequently employed will depend upon the conviction— not only of the psychologist—but of the administration, the school board, and the staff in general that research offers the best possible approach to the improvement of educational quality.

CHAPTER VIII

Organization and Administration
of Psychological Services

The key concept in present-day structure and use of psychological services is adaptability to local requirements. Some of the principal patterns which have emerged through experience are discussed in this chapter. In addition, the conditions under which the school can best profit from the knowledge and skill of the psychologist are suggested.

Structure of Services

The vast heterogeneity of school systems, based on the assumption of local autonomy as most responsive to local need, would lead us to assume that no ideal or preferred form of organizing and administering psychological services has yet evolved. This is precisely the case. Indeed, in small school systems there may be no organization at all, in the formal sense. A psychologist may be assigned to one or more elementary or secondary schools and function as a staff member under the supervision of the principal. Other specialists, such as the remedial reading teacher, the speech therapist, and the nurse, will be coordinate with him as members of the educational team, but all may be directly responsible to the principal. If several psychologists are employed by the same school system and deployed in this manner, they may convene regularly as a "staff" for mutual personal and professional growth. It is a fact that psychologists assigned in this way may function rather differently from school to school in the same system. The question may arise about the organization of the psychologists into a service or department with a responsible head, but the answer is likely to be determined locally. Evidence for a general recommendation about one style of deployment of psychological services over another is not available.

In some school systems, the various specialists offering some kind of personnel service are organized into a department with an administrative head. The members may include psychologists, guidance counselors, visiting teachers, social workers, attendance officers, nurses, and others. Since not all of these staff members offer psychological services, the more common department labels are "personnel services," "special services," "special education," or the like. The administrative head of such a group may be a psychologist by training, but more frequently this is not the case. Many local factors contribute to the decision as to who the administrator shall be. This kind of department under competent leadership has obvious advantages. The members, who carry on some similar as well as different functions, are likely to be brought into regular relationships with one another. One member, the head, has a designated responsibility to perceive the total structure of special services and the interrelation of the various parts. He will probably assume leadership in helping each member develop an appreciation and respect for the competence of others. Roles and functions will be discussed, specified, and implemented in a more harmonious fashion. Specialists may be helped to learn *from* one another as well as *about* one another. None of these values are inherent in the mere fact of organization; the department provides a structure within which leadership may function to realize them. It is probably a fact of organized life that the amount of formal organization is roughly related to the size of the system.

If each specialty were represented by one person, the total number of personnel workers might constitute a rather informal staff with one member assuming administrative leadership. However, special services are not distributed that way. For example, there may be four psychologists and six remedial reading specialists in the group. It may then be considered desirable to designate one person in each of these disciplines to be "chief," with specified powers of control and responsibility over the others. Each "chief" would then be responsible to the department head.

In larger school systems, or in those employing larger numbers in given specialties, this principle may be extended further. There may be, for example, a department of psychological services, consisting only of psychologists, and a guidance department with a head who is responsible to a director (usually an assistant superintendent of schools). In very large cities there may be a department consisting of the mental health professions—psychology, psychiatry, and social work.

The administrative patterns for distributing psychological services should, of course, be based on concepts of how the services are to be rendered to teachers and others. If all the functions advocated for the psychologist in this book are to be provided, a psychologist-pupil ratio of 1:1000 might have to be achieved. The difficulties of stipulating a ratio have already been indicated (see p. 5). The policy of a school in regard to the kinds of services it wants is a basic factor in determining the ratio. Since not all the potential roles outlined herein are the unique province of the psychologist, decisions must be made about other kinds of special services to be employed.

Many of the functions discussed in this book imply a situation in which a psychologist can work rather closely with a small number of teachers and pupils. This requires frequent contact, ready accessibility of services when needed, informal referral procedures, and a minimum of red tape.

In centralized departments, the director of services carries the responsibility for knowing rather intimately the competence and potentialities of his staff, since he should participate at the highest administrative levels in policy discussions about all matters affecting the schools. Since he is accountable for the efficiency of services, continuous evaluation is called for. At times, reports about the kinds and extent of services will have to be prepared.

He also has opportunities to foster the continuing professional development of his staff. The most significant criterion of his effectiveness is the extent to which he successfully releases the creative potential of his staff. A smoothly functioning department is not the goal; it is merely a condition for productive work.

Conditions of Work

The conditions under which a psychologist works have an important bearing upon his effectiveness.

Space. The psychologist should have an office of his own, where all the resources necessary to his functions are at hand for economical use. The physical circumstances must permit privacy and unhurried consideration of problems. The office should be located in or near the traffic lanes used by teachers and pupils, and visibly represent the importance which the school attaches to services. If he serves a school on a rather limited basis, a psychologist may share an office used at other times by other personnel, but there should be one place where equipment, records, and other material may be kept to facilitate his work.

Equipment and records. Minimum equipment for daily work includes cabinets for storage of tests, telephone, dictation machine, and office supplies. Ample reserves of tests frequently used makes for economy in purchase and ready availability. A telephone is a necessity; many problems with parents, teachers, and administrators can be handled by telephone. This may appear obvious, but there are many situations in which time is lost in making contacts, or in which it is assumed that all problems require face-to-face conferences.

It is a waste of professional time for the psychologist to type his own reports, or to write them out in longhand for later typing. In both instances, the result may be less than adequate records because of time pressures, or loss of professional time.

The professional aspects of reports and records have been considered (see Chapter III). Suffice it to say here that files for the housing of confidential records, test protocols, and other materials which are not part of the pupil's regular personnel folder should be provided.

Use of time. It is primarily the responsibility of the psychologist to see that his time is organized for effective service. When school systems discover the values of psychological services, requests are likely to exceed supply and a determination of priorities is essential. Such circumstances provide fertile ground for policy discussions of functions. Are additional services to be sought by adding to staff? Which requests are to be considered more important? After policy decisions are made, the individual is responsible for the efficient use of time. With experience, the psychologist can make reasonable predictions about use of time, so that waiting lists do not develop and unmet requests do not pile up.

Questions do arise at times about the assignment of the psychologist to lunchroom duty, to the accompaniment of pupils on trips, or to the classroom as a substitute teacher. The governing principle to keep in mind is the best employment of professional skill which is in very short supply in most school systems. In emergency situations, judgment must be reserved to the persons involved.

The total hours for employment can no more be specified for the psychologist than they can for the teachers or other professional personnel. Psychologists often use after-school hours for consultations with teachers, committee meetings, and the like. In some communities, psychologists are finding it extremely valuable to make time available in the evening to consult with parents who are not available during working hours. One psychologist who works in a suburb where almost all fathers commute to the city reported considerable success in reaching otherwise recalcitrant fathers by meeting with them early in the morning or during evening hours.

Salary. Salaries for school psychologists vary widely throughout the country. In a profession in which training varies from less than a master's degree to postdoctoral study, variations are to be expected. Qualifications, training, and experience are significant factors. In a given locale, competition with other employment opportunities may be a factor.

In some school systems the teachers' salary guide is used, with appropriate recognition for training, experience, and responsibility; in other systems a separate schedule is developed. Psychologists usually have more training than teachers, with the result that their average salaries are higher.

CHAPTER IX

Future Perspectives

As a profession, school psychology is struggling toward maturity. Opportunities for service far exceed the present capacity for fulfillment. Present trends suggest that demands for more and better services will increase. The profession looks upon the claims which society lays upon it and is both exhilarated and dismayed. Excitement flows from a recognition of the great potential of psychology for improving the quality of education. But an examination of school psychology's readiness to meet the challenges yields an impressive array of problems and some apprehension.

Until very recently, school psychologists functioned as individual professional persons, discharging their roles as competently as they could, but without a sense of collective responsibility for directing the evolution of a profession. In the past decade, a significant change has occurred. A sense of urgency led to the Thayer Conference, the first comprehensive soul-searching to take place in the profession. Since then, local and state associations have emerged to face the problems of professional identity. The national association has grown in size and leadership. These groups have begun to formulate the problems which will have to be solved before school psychology can achieve full maturity as a profession.

School psychology will not meet the challenges which lie ahead through its own efforts only. Educators, representatives of the larger community, and colleagues from other specialties within psychology must become involved in finding solutions. The thesis here, however, is that school psychology must lead the way.

Manpower Shortage

School psychology must recruit into its ranks more young men and women with the talent to become highly qualified psychologists and the desire to use their competence in the service of education. In so doing, it must compete with other professions in placing before young people a bold conception of public service, excellent training facilities, and the challenge to contribute to the growing stature of a profession.

Although there are many more job opportunities than persons to fill them, numbers alone will not be enough. The search for more creative ways to apply psychological knowledge and skill must go on. In this context, the present diversity of roles and widespread experimentation may be a great advantage. But diversity alone does not provide insight or a sense of direction; it must be evaluated and its consequences tested critically with an eye to revision where indicated.

Education and Training

During the past few years, an encouraging number of colleges and universities have established programs for preparing school psychologists. As recently as 1954 there were very few programs of high quality. Even at the present time we have no authoritative evidence of the extent and quality of training programs on a nationwide basis.

Accreditation of training programs lies ahead; it cannot be accomplished until reasonable agreements are reached about the objectives and content of training. Each program today is based upon the concepts of those who conduct it, with due regard for state certification standards where they exist.

A formidable issue in training is the lack of financial support. As expectations rise, costs rise too, and it becomes more difficult for students to finance their preparation without subsidy. This problem is closely tied to the issue of approved standards, for supporting agencies are not disposed to subsidize training unless a profession has developed clearly agreed upon standards.

Standards of training, educational facilities, and sources of financial support for careers in school psychology have high priority in the profession. In addition, resources must be developed for the inservice development of psychologists on the job. Increasing demands for services and expansion in role expectations have left many practitioners in need of further training to meet new responsibilities. Steady upgrading of minimum competence in an ongoing profession is a challenging task indeed. Fortunately, professional organizations of school psychologists, state departments of education, and universities are beginning to realize the need and to take steps to meet it.

Certification Standards

Few, if any, states now have certification standards commensurate with job demands and the conceptions of training embodied in the best training programs today. The national association of school psychologists is providing leadership in developing standards for certification for the guidance of states seeking to establish or improve standards. It will take many years before all states have certification standards with uniformly high expectations.

Epilogue

For school psychology the best is yet to come. The accelerating pace of world events has projected education into a central role in the struggle for survival. No matter what form educational purpose, content, and method may take, considerable reliance will be placed upon psychology to provide knowledge, insight, and skill to participate in the whole range of educational endeavor. School psychology will be called upon to assume a major part in the unfolding drama. Will it be ready?

The roles depicted in this presentation suggest one view of its possibilities. Some of the descriptions portray present reality; others reflect promising directions now being explored in various places, others may be "the stuff that dreams are made of."

The growing self-consciousness of the profession about its problems is already being transformed into determined efforts to find solutions for them. There is reason to believe that school psychology will effectively cope with its problems and move steadily toward a professional maturity that will contribute significantly to its raison d'etre: the continuing improvement of educational opportunity for all children and youth.

Bibliography

Allen, Frederick H., *Psychotherapy with Children*. New York: W. W. Norton & Company, Inc., 1942.

Almy, Millie, *Ways of Studying Children*. New York: Teachers College, Columbia University, 1959.

Blair, Glenn M., *Diagnostic and Remedial Teaching*. New York: The Macmillan Company, 1956.

Bower, Eli M., *The School Psychologist*. Bulletin of the California State Department of Education, Vol. XXIV, No. 12 (November, 1955).

Cunningham, Ruth, *Understanding Group Behavior of Boys and Girls*. New York: Teachers College, Columbia University, 1951.

Cutts, Norma E., *School Psychologists at Mid-Century*. Washington, D.C.: American Psychological Association, Inc., 1955.

Driscoll, Gertrude P., *Child Guidance in the Classroom*. New York: Teachers College, Columbia University, 1955.

Ginott, Haim G., *Group Psychotherapy with Children*. New York: McGraw-Hill Book Co., 1961.

Gottsegen, Monroe G. and Gloria B. Gottsegen, eds., *Professional School Psychology*. New York: Grune & Stratton, Inc., 1960.

Group for the Advancement of Psychiatry, *The Diagnostic Process in Child Psychiatry*, Report No. 38, New York (1957).

Henry, Nelson B., ed., *Mental Health in Modern Education*, Fifty-Fourth Yearbook, Part II. Chicago: National Society for the Study of Education, 1955.

Jahoda, Marie, *Current Concepts of Positive Mental Health*. New York: Basic Books, Inc., 1958.

Jersild, Arthur T., *When Teachers Face Themselves*. New York: Teachers College, Columbia University, 1955.

Krugman, Morris, ed., *Orthopsychiatry and the School*. New York: American Orthopsychiatric Association, 1958.

Marzolf, Stanley S., *Psychological Diagnosis and Counseling in the Schools*. New York: Holt, Rinehart & Winston, Inc., 1956.

Miles, Matthew B., *Learning to Work in Groups*. New York: Teachers College, Columbia University, 1959.

Prescott, Daniel A., *The Child in the Educative Process*. New York: McGraw-Hill Book Co., 1957.

Robinson, Reginald, David F. DeMarche, and Mildred K. Wagle, *Community Resources in Mental Health*. New York: Basic Books, Inc., 1960.

Sivers, William A., Jr. and Raymond D. Salman, *The School Psychologist in Action*. New York: The University of the State of New York, The State Education Department, 1961.

Slavson, S. R., *Child-Centered Group Guidance of Parents*. New York: International Universities Press, 1958.

Strang, Ruth, *Group Work in Education*. New York: Harper & Row, Publishers, 1958.

Tyler, Leona E., *The Work of the Counselor*. New York: Appleton-Century-Crofts, 1953.

White, Mary Alice and Myron W. Harris, *The School Psychologist*. New York: Harper & Row, Publishers, 1961.

Index

Index

114 INDEX

Grouping of pupils, 41
Guidance counselors, 15

H

Historical development:
Binet, 2
child guidance clinics, 3
educational change, 4
Galton, 2
mental hygiene movement, 3
Witmer clinic, 2
Hodges, W. L., 8
House-Tree-Person test, 34

I

Interviews, 30-34
with parents, 33-34
with teachers, 31-33

J

Juvenile conference committee, 80-81

L

Learning as remedial concept, 43

M

Mental health association, 79-80
Mental health consultation (*see* Consultation)

P

Parents:
assessment role, 33-34
consultation role, 74-75
counseling for, 75
education of, 75-76
parent-teacher association, 74
remedial role, 51-53
teacher-parent conference, 76
Personnel functions, 69-70
Play techniques:
in assessment, 31
in therapy, 47
Professional associations, 16-17
Psychiatry:
consultation, psychiatric, 15
role in schools, 73-74
Psychological services:
administrative patterns, 101-103
conditions of work, 103

Psychological services (*Cont.*)
equipment and records, 104
expansion of, 5-6
salary schedules, 105
staff development, 91-92
structure, 101
use of time, 104
Psychotherapy (*see* Remedial)
Pupil:
counseling, 46-47
peer relationships, 49-50, 52
problems, 26-29
pupil-psychologist ratio, 5, 12

R

Reading:
consultant, 15, 41
remedial, 57-58
Records, 39-40, 104
Referral, 24-28
forms for, 24
sources of, 24
teacher role, 24-28
types of, 26
Remedial:
group procedures:
classroom, 54-56
counseling and therapy, 58-60
introduction of, 60
remedial groups, 56-58
individual procedures:
counseling, 46-48
environmental change, 52-53
peer relationships, 49-50
work with parents, 51-52
work with pupils, 46-50
work with teachers, 50-51, 67-68
principles and concepts, 42-45
reading, 57-58
Reports:
to agencies, 40-41
characteristics of, 40
preparation of, 104
purpose of, 40
to teachers, 40
Research:
action, 95-97
consultation, 97-98
educational problems, 93-95
services:
dropouts, study of, 100
group testing norms, 99
reviews of research, 99
Robinson, R., 12
Rorschach test, 34